the
dog who
healed
a family

the
dog who
healed
a family

And Other True Animal
Stories That Warm the
Heart & Touch the Soul

Jo Coudert

HARLEQUIN®

The Dog Who Healed a Family

ISBN-13: 978-0-373-89230-3

Copyright © 2010 by Jo Coudert

Library of Congress Cataloging-in-Publication Data Coudert, Jo.
The dog who healed a family : and other true animal stories that warm the heart and touch the soul / Jo Coudert. p. cm.
ISBN 978-0-373-89230-3 (pbk.)
1. Pets-Anecdotes. 2. Pet owners-Anecdotes. 3. Animals-Anecdotes. 4. Human-animal relationships-Anecdotes. I. Title.
SF416.C68 2010
636.088'7-dc22   2010009073

The following stories appeared originally in *The Reader's Digest*: "Goose Steps," "The Pig Who Loved People," "The Good Shepherd," "I Love You, Pat Myers," "Sister Smog and the Windshield Viper," "An Experiment in Love" and "Frankie Buck."
The following stories appeared originally in *Woman's Day*: "The Dog Who Healed a Family," "Woman (and Dog) to the Rescue," "Connie and the Dog," "How Do You Spank a Duck?" "Where's Bubba?" "Saving Trouper" and "A Swan Called Porcelain."
"Sweet Elizabeth" appeared originally in *McCall's*. "The Puppy Express" appeared originally in *Family Circle*.

www.eHarlequin.com

Printed in U.S.A.

Contents

Preface

All the stories in this book are about animals, and all are true. What the stories have in common is the love and caring that can exist between animals and people. Nancy Topp struggled for weeks to get a seventeen-year-old dog home across fifteen hundred miles. Gene Fleming fashioned shoes for a goose born without feet and supported the goose in a harness until he learned to walk. Months after their javelina disappeared, Patsy and Buddy Thorne were still roaming ranch lands in Texas, Bubba's favorite chocolate in their pockets, searching for their wild pig.

The Thornes recently sent a clipping from their local newspaper describing how a group of men out hunting with bows and arrows came upon a javelina. The animal stood still, gazing at the men, while they shot at it three times. When all three arrows failed to strike home, one of the men ventured close enough to pet the animal and found it was tame and welcomed the attention.

What is amazing about the report is not that the animal was Bubba—it was not—but that the hunters shot three times at a creature that was not big enough or wild enough to be a threat to them and that did not provide sport by running. And because the meat of a javelina is too strong-tasting to be palatable, they were not interested in it for food.

The hunters shot at the javelina because it was there, which is the same reason a neighbor who lives downriver from me catches all the trout within hours of the time the state fish and wildlife service stocks the stream. An amiable man who loves his grandchildren, the neighbor has built the children a tree platform where they can sit silently and shoot at the deer who come to the river to drink at twilight. He also sets muskrat traps in the river and runs over woodchucks and possums on the road.

The family doesn't eat the deer; the frozen body of a doe has been lying all winter in the field in back of my woods. Nor does anyone eat the trout the man catches; he tosses them into a little pond on his property where they stay until they become too numerous and die from lack of oxygen. When I once asked this ordinary, pleasant fellow why he'd gone out of his way to run over a raccoon crossing the road, he looked at me in surprise. "It's an animal!" he said as though that quite explained it.

To many people it is sufficient explanation. After all, did not Jehovah tell Noah and his sons that all the beasts of the earth and fish of the sea were delivered into the hands of man? Surely this is a license to destroy them even if we have no better reason at the time than the fact that they exist and we wish to.

Or is it? Belatedly we are beginning to realize that the duality of people and animals, us and them, is false, just as we have discovered that there is no split between us and the world. The world is us and we are the world. We cannot simply exploit and destroy, either the world or the animals in it, if we are not at the same time to do ourselves irreparable harm.

Consider what a Native American, Chief Seattle, said in 1854: "What is man without the beasts? If all the beasts were gone, man would die from a great loneliness of spirit. For whatever happens to the beasts, soon happens to man. All things are connected. This we know: The Earth does not belong to man; man belongs to the Earth. This we know: All things are connected like the blood which unites one family. All things are connected. Whatever befalls the Earth befalls the sons of the Earth. Man did not weave the web of life. He is merely a strand in it. Whatever he does to the web, he does to himself."

The world belongs to the animals just as much as to us. Let us be unselfish enough to share it with them openly and generously. Which is to say, when you come upon a lost dog or an orphaned fawn or a goose born without feet, give it nothing to fear from you, grant it safety, offer to help if you can, be kind. In return, as the stories here show, you will sometimes find a welcome companionship, and surprisingly often love.

Jo Coudert
Califon, New Jersey

The Puppy Express

Curled nose to tail, the little dog was drowsing in Nancy Topp's lap as the truck rolled along the interstate. Suddenly Nancy felt her stiffen into alertness. "What's the matter, old girl?" Nancy asked. At seventeen, Snoopy had a bit of a heart condition and some kidney problems, and the family was concerned about her.

Struggling to her feet, the dog stared straight ahead. She was a small dog, with a dachshund body but a beagle head, and she almost seemed to be pointing. Nancy followed the dog's intent gaze, and then she saw it, too. A wisp of smoke was curling out of a crack in the dashboard. "Joe!" she shouted at her husband at the wheel. "Joe, the engine's on fire!"

Within seconds the cab of the ancient truck was seething with smoke. Nancy and Joe and their two children—Jodi, twelve, and Matthew, fifteen—leaped to the shoulder of the road and ran. When they were well clear, they turned and waited for the explosion that would blow everything they owned sky-high. Instead, the engine coughed its way into silence, gave a last convulsive shudder and died.

Joe was the first to speak. "Snoopy," he said to the little brown and white dog, "you may not hear or see so good, but there's nothing wrong with your nose."

"Now if you could just tell us how we're going to get home," Matthew joked. Except it wasn't much of a joke. Here they were, fifteen hundred miles from home, stranded on a highway in Wyoming, with the truck clearly beyond even Joe's gift for repairs. The little dog, peering with cataract-dimmed eyes around the circle of faces, seemed to reflect their anxiety.

The Topps were on the road because five months earlier a nephew had told Joe there was work to be had in the Napa Valley and Joe and Nancy decided to take a gamble on moving out there. Breaking up their home in Fort Wayne, Indiana, they packed up the kids and Snoopy and set out for California. But once there, the warehousing job Joe hoped for did not materialize, Nancy and the kids were sharply homesick and their funds melted away. Now it was January and, the gamble lost, they were on their way back home to Fort Wayne.

The truck had gotten them as far as Rock Springs, Wyoming, but now there was nothing to do but sell it to a junk dealer for $25 and hitch a ride to the bus station. Two pieces of bad news greeted them there. Four tickets to Fort Wayne came to more money than they had, much more, and dogs were not allowed on the bus.

"But we've got to take Snoopy with us," Nancy pleaded with the ticket seller, tears welling in her eyes. It had been a disastrous day, but this was the worst news of all.

Joe drew her away from the window. It was no use getting upset about Snoopy, he told her, until they figured out how to get themselves on the bus. With no choice but to ask for help, they called Travelers Aid, and with kind efficiency the local representative arranged for a motel room for them for the night. There, with their boxes and bags piled in a corner, they put in a call to relatives back home, who promised to get together money for the fare and wire it the next day.

"But what about Snoopy?" Matthew said as soon as his father hung up the phone.

"We can't go without Snoopy," Jodi stated flatly.

Joe picked up the little dog. "Snoopy," he said, tugging her floppy ears in the way she liked, "I think you're going to have to hitchhike."

"Don't tease, Joe," Nancy said curtly.

"I'm not teasing, honey," he assured her, and tucked Snoopy into the crook of his arm. "I'm going to try to find an eastbound truck to take the old girl back for us."

At the local truck stop, Joe sat Snoopy on a stool beside him while he fell into conversation with drivers who stopped to pet her. "Gee, I'd like to help you out," one after another said. "She's awful cute and I wouldn't mind the company, but I'm not going through Fort Wayne this trip." The only driver who might have taken her picked Snoopy up and looked at her closely. "Naw," the man growled, "with an old dog like her, there'd be too many pit stops. I got to make time." Still hopeful, Joe tacked up a sign asking for a ride for Snoopy and giving the motel's phone number.

"Somebody'll call before bus time tomorrow," he predicted to the kids when he and Snoopy got back to the motel.

3

"But suppose nobody does?" Jodi said.

"Sweetie, we've got to be on that bus. The Travelers Aid can only pay for us to stay here one night."

The next day Joe went off to collect the wired funds while Nancy and the kids sorted through their possessions, trying to decide what could be crammed into the six pieces of luggage they were allowed on the bus and what had to be left behind. Ordinarily Snoopy would have napped while they worked, but now her eyes followed every move Nancy and the children made. If one of them paused to think, even for a minute, Snoopy nosed at the idle hand, asking to be touched, to be held.

"She knows," Jodi said, cradling her. "She knows something awful is going to happen."

The Travelers Aid representative arrived to take the belongings they could not pack, for donation to the local thrift shop. A nice man, he was caught between being sympathetic and being practical when he looked at Snoopy. "Seventeen is really old for a dog," he said gently. "Maybe you just have to figure she's had a long life and a good one." When nobody spoke, he took a deep breath. "If you want, you can leave her with me and I'll have her put to sleep after you've gone."

The children looked at Nancy but said nothing; they understood there wasn't any choice, and they didn't want to make it harder on their mother by protesting. Nancy bowed her head. She thought of all the walks, all the romps, all the picnics, all the times she'd gone in to kiss the children good-night and Snoopy had lifted her head to be kissed, too.

"Thank you," she told the man. "It's kind of you to offer. But no. No," she repeated firmly. "Snoopy's part of the family, and families don't give up on each other." She reached for the telephone book, looked up kennels in the yellow pages and began dialing. Scrupulously she started each call with the explanation that the family was down on their luck. "But," she begged, "if you'll just keep our little dog until we can find a way to get her to Fort Wayne, I give you my word we'll pay. Please trust me. Please."

A veterinarian with boarding facilities agreed finally to take her, and the Travelers Aid representative drove them to her office. Nancy was the last to say goodbye. She knelt to take Snoopy's frosted muzzle in her hands. "You know we'd never leave you if we could help it," she whispered, "so don't give up. Don't you dare give up. We'll get you back somehow, I promise."

Once back in Fort Wayne, the Topps found a mobile home to rent, one of Joe's brothers gave them his old car, sisters-in-law provided pots and pans and bed linens, the children returned to their old schools and Nancy and Joe found jobs. Bit by bit the family got itself together. But the circle had a painful gap in it. Snoopy was missing. Every day Nancy telephoned a different moving company, a different trucking company, begging for a ride for Snoopy. Every day Jodi and Matthew came through the door asking if she'd had any luck and she had to say no.

By March they'd been back in Fort Wayne six weeks and Nancy was in despair. She dreaded hearing from Wyoming that Snoopy had died out there, never knowing how hard they'd tried to get her back. One day a friend suggested she call the Humane Society. "What good would that do?" Nancy said. "Aren't they only concerned about abandoned animals?" But she had tried everything else, so she telephoned Rod Hale, the director of the Fort Wayne Department of Animal Control, and told him the story.

"I don't know what I can do to help," Rod Hale said when she finished. "But I'll tell you this. I'm sure going to try." A week later, he had exhausted the obvious approaches. Snoopy was too frail to be shipped in the unheated baggage compartment of a plane. A professional animal transporting company wanted $655 to bring her east. Shipping companies refused to be responsible for her. Rod hung up from his latest call and shook his head. "I wish the old-time Pony Express was still in existence," he remarked to his assistant, Skip Cochrane. "They'd have passed the dog along from one driver to another and delivered her back home."

"It'd have been a Puppy Express," Skip joked.

Rod thought for a minute. "By golly, that may be the answer." He got out a map and a list of animal shelters in Wyoming, Nebraska, Iowa, Illinois and Indiana, and picked up the phone. Could he enlist enough volunteers to put together a Puppy Express to transport Snoopy by stages across five states? Would people believe it mattered enough for a seventeen-year-old dog to be reunited with her family that they'd drive a hundred or so miles west to pick her up and another hundred or so miles east to deliver her to the next driver?

In a week he had his answer, and on Sunday, March 11, he called the Topps. "How are you?" he asked Nancy.

"I'd feel a lot better if you had some news for me."

"Then you can begin feeling better right now," Rod told her jubilantly. "The Puppy Express starts tomorrow. Snoopy's coming home!"

Monday morning, in Rock Springs, Dr. Pam McLaughlin checked Snoopy worriedly. The dog had been sneezing the day before. "Look here, old girl," the vet lectured as she took her temperature, "you've kept your courage up until now. This is no time to get sick just when a lot of people are about to go to a lot of trouble to get you back to your family."

Jim Storey, the animal control officer in Rock Springs, had volunteered to be Snoopy's first driver. When he pulled up outside the clinic, Dr. McLaughlin bundled Snoopy in a sweater and carried her to the car. "She's got a cold, Jim," the vet said, "so keep her warm. Medicine and instructions and the special food for her kidney condition are in the shopping bag."

"She's got a long way to go," Jim said. "Is she going to make it?"

"I wish I could be sure of it," the doctor admitted. She put the little dog on the seat beside Jim and held out her hand. Snoopy placed her paw in it. "You're welcome, old girl," the vet said, squeezing it. "It's been a pleasure taking care of you. The best of luck. Get home safely."

Jim and Snoopy drove 108 miles to Rawlings, Wyoming. There they rendezvoused with Cathy English, who had come 118 miles from Casper to meet them. Cathy laughed when she saw Snoopy. "What a funny-looking, serious little creature you are to be traveling in such style," she teased. "Imagine, private chauffeurs across five states." But that evening, when she phoned Rod Hale to report that Snoopy had arrived safely in Casper, she called her "a dear old girl" and admitted that "If she were mine, I'd go to a lot of trouble to get her back, too."

Snoopy went to bed at Cathy's house—a nondescript little brown and white animal very long in the tooth—and woke the next morning a celebrity. Word of the seventeen-year-old dog with a bad cold who was being shuttled across mid-America to rejoin her family had gotten to the news media. After breakfast, dazed by the camera and lights but, as always, polite, Snoopy sat on a desk at the Casper Humane Society and obligingly cocked her head to show off the new leash that was a gift from Cathy. And that night, in Fort Wayne, the Topps were caught between laughter and tears as they saw their old girl peer out at them from the television set.

With the interview behind her, Snoopy set out for North Platte, 350 miles away, in the company of Myrtie Bain, a Humane Society official in Casper who had volunteered for the longest single hop on Snoopy's journey. The two of them stopped overnight in Alliance, and Snoopy, taking a stroll before turning in, got a thorn in her paw. Having come to rely on the kindness of strangers, she held quite still while Myrtie removed it, and then continued to limp until Myrtie accused her of doing it just to get sympathy. Her sneezes, however, were genuine, and Myrtie put her to bed early, covering her with towels to keep off drafts.

In North Platte at noon the next day, more reporters and cameramen awaited them, but as soon as she'd been interviewed, Snoopy was back on the road for a 138-mile trip to Grand Island. Twice more that day she was passed along, arriving in Lincoln, Nebraska, after dark and so tired that she curled up in the first doggie bed she spotted despite the growls of its rightful owner.

In the morning her sneezing was worse and she refused to drink any water. Word of this was sent along with her, and as soon as she arrived in Omaha on the next leg, she was checked over by the Humane Society vet, who found her fever had dropped but she was dehydrated. A messenger was dispatched to the nearest store for Gatorade, to the fascination of reporters, who from then on headlined her as "Snoopy, the Gatorade Dog."

With a gift of a new wicker sleeping basket and a note in the log being kept of her journey—"Happy to be part of the chain reuniting Snoopy with her family"—Nebraska passed the little dog on to Iowa. After a change of car and driver in Des Moines, Snoopy sped on and by nightfall was in Cedar Rapids. Pat Hubbard, in whose home she spent the night, was sufficiently concerned about her to set an alarm and get up three times in the night to force-feed her Gatorade. Snoopy seemed stronger in the morning, and the Puppy Express rolled on.

As happens to travelers, Snoopy's outfit grew baggy and wrinkled, her sweater stretching so much that she tripped on it with almost every step. This did not go unnoticed, and by the time she reached Davenport, she was sporting a new sweater, as well as a collection of toys, food and water dishes and her own traveling bag to carry them in. The log, in addition to noting when she had been fed and walked, began to fill with comments in the margin: "Fantastic little dog!" "What a luv!" "Insists on sitting in the front seat, preferably in a lap." "Likes the radio on." "Hate to give her up! Great companion!"

At nightfall of her fifth and last full day on the road, Snoopy was in Chicago, her next-to-last stop. Whether it was that she was getting close to home or just because her cold had run its course, she was clearly feeling better. Indeed, the vet who examined her told the reporters, "For an old lady who's been traveling all week and has come more than thirteen hundred miles, she's in grand shape. She's going to make it home tomorrow just fine." The Topps, watching the nightly update of Snoopy's journey on the Fort Wayne TV stations, broke into cheers.

The next day was Saturday, March 17. In honor of St. Patrick's Day, the little dog sported a new green coat with a green derby pinned to the collar. The Chicago press did one last interview with her, and then Snoopy had nothing to do but nap until Skip Cochrane arrived from Fort Wayne to drive her the 160 miles home.

Hours before Snoopy and Skip were expected in Fort Wayne, the Topps were waiting excitedly at the Humane Society. Jodi and Matthew worked on a room-sized banner that read "Welcome Home, Snoopy! From Rock Springs, Wyoming, to Fort Wayne, Indiana, via the Puppy Express," with her route outlined across the bottom and their signatures in the corner. Reporters from the Fort Wayne TV stations and newspapers, on hand to report the happy ending to Snoopy's story, interviewed the Topps and the shelter's staff, in particular Rod Hale, whose idea the Puppy Express had been. One interviewer asked him why the volunteers had done it. Why had thirteen staff members of ten Humane Societies and animal shelters gone to so much trouble for one little dog?

Rod told him what one volunteer had said to him on the phone. "It would have been so easy to tell Nancy Topp that nothing could be done. Instead, you gave all of us a chance to make a loving, caring gesture. Thank you for that."

Somewhere amid the fuss and confusion, Rod found time to draw Nancy aside and give her word that Snoopy would be arriving home with her boarding bill marked "Paid." An anonymous friend of the Humane Society in Casper had taken care of it.

"I thought I was through with crying," Nancy said as the warm tears bathed her eyes. "Maybe it was worth our little dog and us going through all this just so we'd find out how kind people can be."

The CB radio crackled and Skip Cochrane's voice filled the crowded room. "Coming in! The Puppy Express is coming in!"

Nancy and Joe and the children rushed out in the subfreezing air, the reporters on their heels. Around the corner came the pickup truck, lights flashing, siren sounding. "Snoopy's here!" shouted the children. "Snoopy's home!"

And there the little dog was, sitting up on the front seat in her St. Patrick's Day outfit, peering nearsightedly out of the window at all the commotion. After two months of separation from her family, after a week on the road, after traveling across five states for fifteen hundred miles in the company of strangers, Snoopy had reached the end of her odyssey.

Nancy got to the truck first. In the instant before she snatched the door open, Snoopy recognized her. Barking wildly, she scrambled into Nancy's arms. Then Joe was there, and the children. Laughing, crying, they hugged Snoopy and each other. The family that didn't give up on even its smallest member was back together again.

Sweet Elizabeth

Jane Bartlett first saw the white rabbit in a pet shop window at Easter time. The other rabbits were jostling for places at a bowl of chow, but this one was sitting up on her haunches, gazing solemnly back at the faces pressed against the glass staring at her. One ear stood up stiff and straight, as a proper rabbit's ear should, but the other flopped forward over one eye, making her look as raffish as a little old lady who has taken a drop too much and knocked her hat askew.

An executive of the company in which Jane was a trainee came by, stopped to say hello and chuckled at the sight of the rabbit. Mr. Corwin was a friendly, fatherly man, and as they stood there smiling at the funny-looking creature, Jane found herself telling him stories about Dumb Bunny, the white rabbit she'd had as a small child who drank coffee from her father's breakfast cup and once leaped after a crumb in the toaster, singeing his whiskers into tight little black corkscrews. Some of the homesickness Jane was feeling at being new in New York City must have been in her voice, for on Easter morning her doorbell rang and a deliveryman handed her a box.

She set it on the floor while she read the card, and Robert, her tomcat, always curious about packages, strolled over to sniff it. Suddenly he crouched, tail twitching, ready to spring. Jane cautiously raised the lid of the box and up popped the rabbit with the tipsy ear. The cat hissed fiercely. Peering nearsightedly at him, the rabbit shook her head, giving herself a resounding thwack in the nose with her floppy ear, hopped out of the box and made straight for the cat. He retreated. She pressed pleasantly forward. He turned and fled. She pursued. He jumped up on a table. She looked dazedly around, baffled by the disappearance of her newfound friend.

Jane picked her up to console her, and the rabbit began nuzzling her arm affectionately. "Don't try to butter me up," Jane told her sternly. "A city apartment is no place for a rabbit. You're going straight back to the pet shop tomorrow." The rabbit was a tiny creature, her bones fragile under her skin, her fur as white as a snowfield and soft as eiderdown. Gently Jane tugged the floppy ear upright, then let it slip like velvet through her fingers. How endearing the white rabbit was. Could she possibly… Jane shifted her arm and discovered a hole as big as a half-dollar chewed in the sleeve of her sweater. "That does it," Jane said, hastily putting the rabbit down. "You've spoiled your chances." With a mournful shake of her head, the rabbit hopped off in search of the cat.

Jane had a careful speech planned when she arrived at her office the next morning, but the kind executive looked so pleased with himself that the words went out of her head. "What have you named her?" he asked, beaming. She said the first thing that came to mind: "Elizabeth."

"Sweet Elizabeth," he said. "Wonderful!"

Sweet Elizabeth, indeed. Jane was tempted to tell him that Sweet Elizabeth had dined on her best sweater and spent the night in the bathroom, where she had pulled the towels off the racks and unraveled the toilet paper to make a nest for herself. Instead, she began to describe the rabbit's crush on Robert the cat, and soon half the office had gathered around, listening and laughing. It was the first time anyone had paid the least bit of attention to her, and Jane began to wonder whether she wasn't being too hasty about getting rid of Elizabeth. She did go to the pet shop on her lunch hour, however, just to sound them out. Their no-return policy was firm. The best they would do was sell Jane a wooden cage painted to look like a country cottage to keep the rabbit in.

"Don't get the wrong idea," she told Elizabeth that evening as she settled her into it. "It's just temporary until I find a home for you."

In the night it wasn't the sound of the rabbit butting off the roof of the cottage that awakened Jane. She slept through that. It was the crash of the ficus tree going over when Sweet Elizabeth, having nibbled away the tasty lower leaves, went after the higher ones. The next day Jane bought a latch for the cottage. That night Elizabeth worked it loose and ate the begonias on the windowsill. The following day Jane bought a lock. That night Elizabeth gnawed a new front door in her cottage.

It was not hunger or boredom that fueled Elizabeth's determination to get loose; it was her passion for Robert. The minute Jane let her out, she hopped to him and flung herself down between his paws. He, of course, boxed her soundly for her impertinence, but her adoration wore him down, and one day he pretended to be asleep when she lay down near enough to touch him with one tiny white paw. Soon, as though absentmindedly, he was including her in his washups, with particular attention paid to the floppy ear where it had dusted along the floor.

All of this made marvelous stories for Jane to tell in the office, and she discovered it wasn't so hard to make friends after all. She even began to gain something of a reputation for wit when she described how Robert, finding that Elizabeth did not understand games involving catnip mice, invented a new one for the two of them.

Since Elizabeth followed him about as tenaciously as a pesky kid sister, he could easily lure her out onto Jane's tiny terrace. Then he dashed back inside and hid behind a wastebasket. Slowly Elizabeth would hop to the doorway and peer cautiously about. Not seeing the cat anywhere, she'd jump down the single step, whereupon Robert would pounce, rolling them both over and over across the living room rug until Elizabeth kicked free with her strong hind legs. Punch-drunk from the tumbling about, she'd stagger to her feet, shake herself so that her tipsy ear whirled about her head, then scramble off and happily follow the cat outside again.

This game was not all that Elizabeth learned from Robert. He taught her something far more important, at least from Jane's point of view. Out on the terrace were flower boxes that were much more to Robert's liking than his indoor litter box. Time after time, while Robert scratched in the dirt, Elizabeth watched, her head cocked, her ear swinging gently. She was not a swift thinker, but one day light dawned. Robert stepped out of the flower box and she climbed in, which is how Elizabeth, with a little help from her friend, came to be housebroken.

With that problematic matter taken care of and all the plants eaten to nubbins anyway, Jane gave up trying to confine Elizabeth to her cottage and let her stay free. She met Jane at the door in the evening, just as Robert did, and sat up to have her head patted. She learned her name; she learned what "no" meant if said loudly and accompanied by a finger shaken under her nose; she learned what time meals were served and that food arrived at the apartment in paper bags. When Jane came home with groceries and set a bag even momentarily on the floor, Elizabeth's strong teeth quickly ripped a hole in it. That is, unless she smelled carrots, in which case she tugged the bag onto its side and scrambled into it. If Jane got to the carrots before Elizabeth did and put them away on the bottom shelf of the refrigerator, the rabbit bided her time until Jane opened the door again, then she stood up on her hind legs and yanked the carrots back out. It got so that Jane never dared slam the refrigerator door without first making sure Elizabeth's head was not inside it.

But then dinner would be over, the food put away, and Jane settled down to read in her easy chair. First Robert would come, big and purring and kneading with his paws to make a satisfactory spot for himself in her lap. Then Elizabeth would amble over, sit up on her haunches, her little paws folded primly on her chest, and study the situation to decide where there was room for her. With a flying leap, she'd land on top of Robert, throw herself over and push with her hind legs until she'd managed to wedge herself in between the cat and Jane. Soon the twitching of her nose would slow, then cease, and she would be asleep.

At such times, it was easy for Jane to let her hand stray over the soft fur, to call her Sweet Elizabeth, to forgive her all her many transgressions—the sock chewed into fragments, the gnawed handle on a pocketbook, the magazine torn into scraps. But one day Elizabeth went too far; she chewed the heels off Jane's best pair of shoes. Jane decided she had to go. And she had a prospective family to adopt her: a young couple with three small children. She invited the parents, along with two other couples, to dinner.

All that rolling around on the rug with Robert had turned the white rabbit rather gray, and, wanting Elizabeth to look her most beguiling, Jane decided to give her a bath. She filled a dishpan with warm water and plopped Elizabeth into it. The rabbit sprang out. Jane hustled her back in and this time got a firm grip on her ears. Elizabeth kicked and Jane let go. On the third try, Jane got her thoroughly soaped on the back but Elizabeth's powerful hind legs would not let her near her stomach. Persuading herself that no one would look at the rabbit's underside, Jane rinsed her off as best she could and tried to dry her with a towel. Wet, the rabbit's silky fur matted into intricate knots. Jane brushed; Elizabeth licked. Jane combed; Elizabeth licked. Hours later, Elizabeth's fur was still sticking out in every direction and it was obvious that a soggy mass on her stomach was never going to dry. Afraid Elizabeth would get pneumonia, Jane decided to cut out the worst of the knots. With manicure scissors, she began carefully to snip. To her horror, a hole suddenly appeared. Elizabeth's skin was as thin as tissue paper and the scissors had cut right through it. Jane rushed to get Mercurochrome and dab it on the spot. In the rabbit's wet fur, the Mercurochrome spread like ink on blotting paper. Now Jane had a damp rabbit with a dirty-gray stomach dyed red.

The sight of her sitting up at the door to greet each new arrival sent Jane's guests into gales of laughter, which Elizabeth seemed to enjoy. She hopped busily about to have her ears scratched. Jane was keeping a wary eye on her, of course, and saw the moment Elizabeth spotted the stuffed celery on the hors d'oeuvres tray. But Jane wasn't quite quick enough. Elizabeth leaped and landed in the middle of the tray. Even that simply occasioned more laughter, and there were cries of protest when Jane banished Elizabeth to her cottage.

After dinner, Jane yielded and released her. Quite as though Elizabeth had used the time in her cottage to think up what she might do to entertain the party, she hopped into the exact center of the living room floor and gazed seriously around the circle of faces. When silence had fallen and she had everyone's full attention, she leaped straight into the air, whirled like a dervish and crash-landed in a sprawl of legs and flying ears. The applause was prolonged. Peeping shyly from behind her ear, Elizabeth accepted it, looking quite pleased with herself.

The children's father adored her, and when in the course of the evening he saw that Elizabeth went to the terrace door and scratched to be let out, he couldn't wait to take her home. "She's housebroken," he reminded his wife, who was hesitating, "and the kids'll love her." Elizabeth, returning, climbed into his lap, and it was settled: Elizabeth was to go to her new family. Until the end of the evening. "What have you spilled on yourself?" the man's wife asked. The edge of his suit jacket, from lapel to bottom button, was white. Elizabeth had nibbled it down to the backing.

"You rat," Jane scolded her when the guests had gone. "I found a good home for you, and you blew it." Elizabeth shook her head remorsefully, beating herself with her floppy ear, and wandered away. After Jane had cleaned up the kitchen and was ready for bed, she went looking for Elizabeth to put her in her cottage. She hunted high, low and in between. Where was she? Beginning to be frantic, she went through the apartment a second time. She even looked over the terrace railing, wondering for one wild moment if Elizabeth had been so contrite she'd thrown herself off. Only because there was nowhere else to search did Jane open the refrigerator door. There Elizabeth was, on the bottom shelf, having a late-night snack of carrot sticks and parsley.

For quite a while after that, nothing untoward happened, and Elizabeth, Robert and Jane settled into a peaceful and loving coexistence. When Jane watched Elizabeth sunbathing on the terrace beside Robert or sitting on her haunches to wash her face with her dainty paws or jumping into her lap to be petted, she found herself wondering how she could have imagined giving Elizabeth up. Until the day she did a thorough housecleaning and moved the couch. The rug had been grazed down to the backing.

"She's eating me out of house and home. Literally," Jane wailed to a college friend over lunch. "I'm going to have to turn her in to the ASPCA."

"Don't do that. I'll take her," Jane's friend replied, surprising her because Jane knew she did not approve of pets in the house. "She can live in our garage. Evan's ten now. It'll be good for him to have the responsibility of caring for an animal."

Jane's bluff had been called. Could she really envision life without Sweet Elizabeth? She was silent. Her friend said, "Come on. We'll go get her right now."

Elizabeth met them at the door, sitting up as usual to have her ears scratched. "Oh, she's cute," said the friend, but so perfunctorily that Jane knew she had missed the point of Elizabeth. "Never mind," Jane whispered into Elizabeth's soft fur, "it'll be all right. She'll come to love you, just as I did, and you'll be happy in the country." Elizabeth shook her head slowly. Was there reproach in her eyes? Jane gave one last kiss to that foolish ear.

Robert was restless that evening, going often out on the terrace. "Oh, Robbie," Jane told him, "I'm so sorry. She was your friend, too, and I didn't think of that." As Jane hugged him, the old emptiness returned, the emptiness of the time before Sweet Elizabeth when Jane used to imagine that everyone else's phone was ringing, that everyone else had friends to be with and places to go. A little white rabbit who gave Jane the courage to reach out had made a surprising difference in her life.

It was weeks before she slammed the refrigerator door without a second thought, stopped expecting an innocent white face to come peeking around the terrace door, gave up listening for the thump of those heavy back feet. For a long time she didn't trust herself even to inquire about Elizabeth. Then one day she was driving to

Boston and, on impulse, decided to stop off in Connecticut to see her. No one was home, but the garage door was open. It was some time before Jane's eyes got accustomed to the dark and she could distinguish the white blur that was Elizabeth. The little rabbit was huddled in a corner of her cottage, shaking with cold. The straw on the floor was soaking wet. The draft from the open door was bitter. Her food and water bowls were empty. Jane spoke her name and Elizabeth crept into her arms. Wrapping her in a sweater, Jane canceled her trip to Boston and headed back home.

She called her college friend the next day and told her she'd missed Elizabeth so much that she'd kidnapped her. That was all right, her friend said; what with the basketball season and all, her son hadn't had much time for the rabbit. That left Jane with just one other phone call to make—the one canceling the order for a new rug. Then she settled back to watch Elizabeth and Robert rolling across the floor together.

Frankie Buck

On a narrow road twisting along beside a mountain stream lay a deer, struck and killed by a car.

A motorist happening along the infrequently traveled road swerved to avoid the deer's body. As the driver swung out, he noticed a slight movement and stopped. There, huddled beside the dead doe, was a fawn, a baby who must have been born as its mother died, for the umbilical cord was still attached. "I don't suppose you have a chance," the motorist told the tiny creature as he tied off the cord, "but at least I can take you where it's warm."

The nearest place was the power plant of a state geriatric institution on a wooded mountaintop overlooking the town of Glen Gardner, New Jersey. Maintenance men there quickly gathered rags to make a bed for the fawn behind the boiler. When the fawn tried to suck the fingers reaching out to pet it, the men realized it was hungry and took a rubber glove, pricked pinholes in one finger, diluted some of the evaporated milk they used for their coffee and offered it to the fawn, who drank eagerly.

The talk soon turned to what to name the deer. Jean Gares, a small, spare man who was the electrician at the institution, had a suggestion. "If it's a female, we can call her Jane Doe," he proposed. "If it's a male, Frank Buck." The others laughed and agreed.

With the maintenance men taking turns feeding it around the clock, the little deer's wobbly legs—and its curiosity—soon grew strong enough to bring it out from behind the boiler. The men on their coffee breaks petted and played with the creature, and as soon as they were certain that Frank Buck was the name that fit, they shortened it to Frankie and taught him to answer to it. The only one who didn't call him Frankie, oddly enough, was Jean Gares. He, his voice rough with affection, addressed him as "you little dumb donkey," as in "Come on and eat this oatmeal, you little dumb donkey. I cooked it specially for you."

When Jean came to work at six each morning, always in his right-hand pocket was a special treat, an apple or a carrot, even sometimes a bit of chocolate, which Frankie quickly learned to nuzzle for. On nice days the two of them stepped outside, and Jean rested his hand on Frankie's head and stroked his fur as they enjoyed the morning air together.

At the far end of the field in front of the power plant, deer often came out of the woods to graze in the meadow. When Frankie caught their scent, his head came up and his nose twitched. "We'd better tie him up or we're going to lose him," one of the men commented. Jean shook his head. "He'll know when it's time to go," he said. "And when it is time, that's the right thing for him to do."

The first morning Frankie ventured away from the power plant, it wasn't to join the deer in the meadow but to follow Jean. The two-story white stucco buildings at Glen Gardner were originally built at the turn of the century as a tuberculosis sanitarium and are scattered at various levels about the mountaintop. Cement walks and flights of steps connect them, and Jean was crossing on his rounds from one building to another one morning when he heard the tapping of small hooves behind him. "Go on home, you dumb donkey," he told Frankie sternly. "You'll fall and hurt yourself." But Frankie quickly got the hang of the steps, and from then on the slight, white-haired man in a plaid flannel shirt followed by a delicate golden fawn was a familiar early morning sight.

One day, one of the residents, noticing Frankie waiting by the door of a building for Jean to reappear, opened the door and invited him in. Glen Gardner houses vulnerable old people who have been in state mental hospitals and need special care. When Frankie was discovered inside, the staff rushed to banish him. But then they saw how eagerly one resident after another reached out to touch him.

"They were contact-hungry," says staff member Ruby Durant. "We were supplying marvelous care, but people need to touch and be touched as well." When the deer came by, heads lifted, smiles spread and old people who seldom spoke asked the deer's name. "The whole wing lit up," remembers Ruby. "When we saw that and realized how gentle Frankie was, we welcomed him."

His coming each day was something for the residents to look forward to. When they heard the quick *tap-tap* of Frankie's hooves in the corridor, they reached for the crust, the bit of lettuce or the piece of apple they had saved from their own meals to give him. "He bowed to you when you gave him something," says one of the residents. "That would be," she qualifies solemnly, "if he was in the mood." She goes on to describe how she offered Frankie a banana one day, and after she had peeled it for him, "I expected him to swallow the whole thing, but he started at the top and took little nibbles of it to the bottom, just like you or me."

As accustomed as the staff became to Frankie's presence, nevertheless, when a nurse ran for the elevator one day and found it already occupied by Frankie and a bent, very old lady whom she knew to have a severe heart condition, she was startled. "Pauline," she said nervously, "aren't you afraid Frankie will be frightened and jump around when the elevator moves?"

"He wants to go to the first floor," Pauline said firmly.

"How do you know?"

"I know. Push the button."

The nurse pushed the button. The elevator started down. Frankie turned and faced front. When the doors opened, he strolled out.

"See?" said Pauline triumphantly.

Discovering a line of employees in front of the bursar's window one day, Frankie companionably joined the people waiting to be paid. When his turn at the window came, the clerk peered out at him. "Well, Frankie," she said, "I wouldn't mind giving you a paycheck. You're our best social worker. But who's going to take you to the bank to cash it?"

Frankie had the run of Glen Gardner until late fall, when superintendent Irene Salayi noticed that antlers were sprouting on his head. Fearful he might accidentally injure a resident, she decreed banishment. Frankie continued to frequent the grounds, but as the months passed he began exploring farther afield. An evening came when he did not return to the power plant. He was a year old and on his own.

Every morning, though, he was on hand to greet Jean and explore his pocket for the treat he knew would be there. In the afternoon he would reappear, and residents would join him on the broad front lawn and pet him while he munched a hard roll or an apple. A longtime resident named George, a solitary man with a speech defect who didn't seem to care whether people understood what he said or not, taught Frankie to respond to his voice, and the two of them often went for walks together.

When Frankie was two years old—a sleek creature with six-point antlers and a shiny coat shading from tawny to deepest mahogany—there was an April snowstorm. About ten inches covered the ground when Jean Gares came to work on the Friday before Easter, but that didn't seem enough to account for the fact that for the first time Frankie wasn't waiting for him. Jean sought out George after he'd made his rounds and George led the way to a pair of Norway spruces where Frankie usually sheltered when the weather was bad. But Frankie wasn't there or in any other of his usual haunts, nor did he answer to George's whistle. Jean worried desperately about Frankie during the hunting season, as did everyone at Glen Gardner, but the hunting season was long over. What could have happened to him?

Jean tried to persuade himself that the deep snow had kept Frankie away, but he didn't sleep well that night, and by Saturday afternoon he decided to go back to Glen Gardner and search for him. He got George, and the two of them set out through the woods. It was late in the day before they found the deer. Frankie was lying on a patch of ground where a steam pipe running underneath had thawed the snow. His right front leg was shattered. Jagged splinters of bone jutted through the skin. Dried blood was black around the wound. Jean dropped to his knees beside him. "Oh, you dumb donkey," he whispered, "what happened? Were dogs chasing you? Did you step in a woodchuck hole?" Frankie's eyes were dim with pain, but he knew Jean's voice and tried to lick his hand.

Word that Frankie was hurt flicked like lightning through the center, and residents and staff waited anxiously while Jean made call after call in search of a veterinarian who would come to the mountain on a holiday weekend. Finally one agreed to come, but not until the next day, and by then Frankie was gone from the thawed spot. George tracked him through the snow, and when the vet arrived, he guided Jean and the grumbling young man to a thicket in the woods.

For the vet it was enough just to glimpse Frankie's splintered leg. He reached in his bag for a hypodermic needle to put the deer out of his misery. "No," said Jean, catching his arm. "No. We've got to try to save him."

"There's no way to set a break like that without an operation," the vet said, "and this is a big animal, a wild animal. I don't have the facilities for something like this."

He knew of only one place that might. Exacting a promise from the vet to wait, Jean rushed to the main building to telephone.

Soon he was back with an improvised sled; the Round Valley Veterinary Hospital fifteen miles away had agreed at least to examine Frankie if the deer was brought there. Cradling Frankie's head in his lap, Jean spoke to him quietly until the tranquilizing injection the vet gave him took hold. When the deer drifted into unconsciousness, the three men lifted him onto the sled, hauled him out of the woods and loaded him into Jean's pickup truck.

X-rays at the hospital showed a break so severe that a stainless-steel plate would be needed to repair it. "You'll have to stand by while I operate," Dr. Gregory Zolton told Jean. "I'll need help to move him." Jean's stomach did a flip-flop, but he swallowed hard and nodded.

Jean forgot his fear that he might faint as he watched Dr. Zolton work through the three hours of the operation. "It was beautiful," he remembers, his sweetly lined face lighting up. "So skillful the way he cleaned away the pieces of bone and ripped flesh and skin, then opened Frankie's shoulder and took bone from there to make a bridge between the broken ends and screwed the steel plate in place. I couldn't believe the care he took, but he said a leg that wasn't strong enough to run and jump on wasn't any use to a deer."

After stitching up the incision, Dr. Zolton had orders for Jean. "I want you to stay with him until he's completely out of the anesthetic to make sure he doesn't hurt himself. Also, you've got to give him an antibiotic injection twice a day for the next seven days. I'll show you how."

There was an unused stable on the Glen Gardner grounds. Jean took Frankie there and settled him in a stall, and all night long Jean sat in the straw beside him. "Oh, you dumb donkey," he murmured whenever Frankie stirred, "you got yourself in such a lot of trouble, but it's going to be all right. Lie still. Lie still." And he stroked Frankie's head and held him in his arms when Frankie tried to struggle to his feet. With the soothing, known voice in his ear, Frankie each time fell back asleep, until finally, as the sun was coming up, he came fully awake. Jean gave him water and a little food, and only when he was sure Frankie was not frightened did he take his own stiff bones home to bed.

When word came that Frankie had survived the operation, a meeting of the residents' council at Glen Gardner was called. Ordinarily it met to consider recommendations and complaints it wished to make to the staff, but on this day Mary, who was its elected president, had something different on her mind. "You know as well as I do that there's no operation without a big bill. Now, Frankie's our deer, right?" The residents all nodded. "So it stands to reason we've got to pay his bill, right?" The nods came more slowly.

"How are we going to do that?" Kenneth, who had been a businessman, asked.

After considerable discussion, it was decided to hold a sale of cookies that they would bake in the residents' kitchen. Also, they would take up a collection, with people contributing what they could from their meager earnings in the sheltered workshop or the small general store the patients ran on the premises. "But first, before we do any of that," a resident named Marguerite said firmly, "we have to send Frankie a get-well basket."

The residents' council worked the rest of the day finding a basket, decorating it and making a card. The next day a sack of apples was purchased at the general store and each apple was polished until it shone. Mary, Marguerite and George were deputized to deliver the basket. Putting it in a plastic garbage bag so the apples wouldn't roll down the hill if they slipped in the snow, the three of them set out. They arrived without mishap and quietly let themselves into the stable. Frankie was sleeping in the straw, but he roused when they knelt beside him. Mary read him the card, Marguerite gave him an apple to eat, George settled the basket where he could see it but not nibble it and the three of them returned to the main building to report that Frankie was doing fine and was well pleased with his present.

By the seventh day after the operation, Jean called Dr. Zolton to say it was impossible to catch Frankie and hold him still for the antibiotic injections. Dr. Zolton chuckled. "If he's that lively," he told Jean, "he doesn't need antibiotics." But he warned it was imperative that Frankie be kept inside for eight weeks, for if he ran on the leg before it knit, it would shatter again.

Concerned about what to feed him for that length of time, Jean watched from the windows of his own house in the woods and on the grounds of Glen Gardner to see what the deer were eating. As soon as the deer moved away from a spot, Jean rushed to the place and gathered the clover, alfalfa, honeysuckle vines, young apple leaves—whatever it was the deer had been feeding on. Often George helped him, and each day they filled a twenty-five-pound sack. Frankie polished off whatever they brought, plus whatever residents coming to visit him at the stable had scavenged from their own meals in the way of rolls, carrots, potatoes and fruit.

"We'd go to see him, and oh, he wanted to get out so bad," remembers Marguerite, a roly-poly woman with white hair springing out in an aura around her head. "Always he'd be standing with his nose pressed against a crack in the door. He smelled spring coming, and he just pulled in that fresh air like it was something wonderful to drink."

When the collection, mostly in pennies and nickels, had grown to $135, the council instructed Jean to call Dr. Zolton and ask for his bill so they could determine if they had enough money to pay it. The day the bill arrived, Mary called a council meeting. The others were silent, eyes upon her, as she opened it. Her glance went immediately to the total at the bottom of the page. Her face fell. "Oh, dear," she murmured bleakly, "we owe three hundred and ninety-two dollars." Not until she shifted her bifocals did she see the handwritten notation: "Paid in Full—Gregory Zolton, DVM."

When the eight weeks of Frankie's confinement were up, Mary, Marguerite, George, Jean and Dr. Zolton gathered by the stable door. It was mid-June, and the grass was knee-deep in the meadow. Jean opened the barn door. Frankie had his nose against the crack as usual. He peered out from the interior darkness. "Come on, Frankie," Jean said softly. "You can go now." But Frankie was so used to someone slipping in and quickly closing the door that he didn't move. "It's all right," Jean urged quietly. "You're free." Frankie took a tentative step and looked at Jean. Jean stroked his head. "Go on, Frankie," he said, and gave him a little push.

Suddenly Frankie understood. He exploded into a run, flying over the field as fleetly as a greyhound, his hooves barely touching the ground.

"Slow down, slow down," muttered Dr. Zolton worriedly.

"He's so glad to be out," Mary said wistfully. "I don't think we'll ever see him again."

At the edge of the woods, Frankie swerved. He was coming back! Still as swift as a bird, he flew toward them. Near the stable he wheeled again. Six times he crossed the meadow. Then, flanks heaving, tongue lolling, he pulled up beside them. Frankie had tested his leg to its limits. It was perfect. "Good!" said George distinctly. Everyone cheered.

Soon Frankie was back in his accustomed routine of waiting for Jean by the power plant at six in the morning and searching his pockets for a treat, then accompanying him on at least part of his rounds. At noontime he canvassed the terraces when the weather was fine, for the staff often lunched outdoors. A nurse one day, leaning forward to make an impassioned point, turned back to her salad, only to see the last of it, liberally laced with Italian dressing, vanishing into Frankie's mouth. Whenever a picnic was planned, provision had to be made for Frankie, for he was sure to turn up, and strollers in the woods were likely to hear a light, quick step behind them and find themselves joined for the rest of their walk by a companionable deer. One visitor whom nobody thought to warn became hysterical at what she took to be molestation by a large antlered creature until someone turned her pockets out and gave Frankie the after-dinner mints he had smelled there and of which he was particularly fond.

In the fall, Jean, anticipating the hunting season, put a red braided collar around Frankie's neck. Within a day or two it was gone, scraped off against a tree in the woods. Jean put another on, and it, too, disappeared. "He doesn't like red," Pauline said. "He likes yellow."

"How do you know?"

"I know."

Jean tried yellow. Frankie kept the collar on. Jean was glad of this when Frankie stopped showing up in the mornings. He knew that it was rutting season and it was natural for Frankie to be off in the woods staking out his territory. The mountain was a nature preserve and no hunting was allowed, but still he worried about Frankie because poachers frequently sneaked into the woods; Frankie might wander off the mountain following a doe he fancied.

One day a staff member on her way to work spotted a group of hunters at the base of the mountain. Strolling down the road toward them was Frankie. She got out of her car, turned Frankie around so that he was headed up the mountain, then drove along behind him at five miles an hour. Frankie kept turning to look at her reproachfully, but she herded him with her car until she got him back to safety. On another memorable day, a pickup truck filled with hunters drove up to the power plant. When the tailgate was lowered, Frankie jumped from their midst. The hunters had read about Frankie in the local paper, and when they spotted a tame deer wearing a yellow collar, they figured it must be Frankie and brought him home.

After the rutting season, Frankie reappeared, but this time when he came out of the woods, three does were with him. And that has been true in the years since. The does wait for him at the edge of the lawn, and when he has visited with Jean and made his tour of the terraces and paused awhile under the crab apple tree waiting for

George to shake down some fruit for him, Frankie rejoins the does and the little group goes back into the woods.

Because the hunting season is a time of anxiety for the whole of Glen Gardner until they know Frankie has made it through safely, George and the other people at Glen Gardner debate each fall whether to lock Frankie in the stable for his own safety. The vote always goes against it. The feeling is that Frankie symbolizes the philosophy of Glen Gardner, which is to provide care but not to undermine independence. "A deer and a person, they each have their dignity," Jean says. "It's okay to help them when they need help, but you mustn't take their choices away from them."

So, Frankie Buck, the wonderful deer of Glen Gardner, remains free. He runs risks, of course, but life itself is risky, and if Frankie should happen to get into trouble, he knows where there are friends he can count on.

I Love You, Pat Myers

Pat Myers was returning home after four days in the hospital for tests. "Hi, Casey. I'm back," she called as she unlocked the door of her apartment. Casey, her African gray parrot, sprang to the side of his cage, chattering with excitement. "Hey, you're really glad to see me, aren't you?" Pat teased as Casey bounced along his perch. "Tell me about it."

The parrot drew himself up like a small boy bursting to speak but at a loss for words. He jigged. He pranced. He peered at Pat with one sharp eye, then the other. Finally he hit upon a phrase that pleased him. "Shall we do the dishes?" he exploded happily.

"What a greeting." Pat laughed, opening the cage so Casey could hop onto her hand and be carried to the living room. As she settled in an easy chair, Casey sidled up her arm; Pat crooked her elbow and the bird settled down with his head nestled on her shoulder. Affectionately Pat dusted the tips of her fingers over his velvety gray feathers and scarlet tail. "I love you," she said. "Can you say 'I love you, Pat Myers'?"

Casey cocked an eye at her. "I live on Mallard View."

"I know where you live, funny bird. Tell me you love me."

"Funny bird."

A widow with two married children, Pat had lived alone for some years and devoted her energy to running a chain of dress shops. It was a happy and successful life. Then one evening she was watching television when, without warning, her eyes went out of focus. Innumerable tests later, a diagnosis of arteritis was established. Treatment of the inflammation of an artery in her temple lasted for more than a year and led to an awkward weight gain, swollen legs and such difficulty in breathing that Pat had to give up her business and for months was scarcely able to leave her apartment, which more and more grew to feel oppressively silent and empty. Always an outgoing, gregarious woman, Pat was reluctant to admit, even to her daughter, just how lonely she was, but finally she broke down and confessed, "Annie, I'm going nuts here by myself. What do you think—should I advertise for someone to live with me?"

"That's such a lottery," her daughter said. "How about a pet?"

"I've thought of that, but I haven't the strength to walk a dog, I'm allergic to cats and fish don't have a whole lot to say."

"Birds do," said her daughter. "Why not a parrot?"

That struck Pat as possibly a good idea, and she telephoned an ornithologist to ask his advice. After ruling out a macaw as being too big and a cockatoo or cockatiel as possibly triggering Pat's allergies, he recommended an African gray, which he described as the most accomplished talker among parrots. Pat and Annie visited a breeder and were shown two little featherless creatures huddled together for warmth. The breeder explained that the eggs were hatched in an incubator and the babies kept separate from their parents so that they would become imprinted on humans and make excellent pets. "After your bird's been with you for a while," the breeder assured Pat, "he'll think you're his mother."

"I'm not sure I want to be the mother of something that looks like a plucked chicken," Pat said doubtfully. But Annie persuaded her to put a deposit down on the bird with the brightest eyes, and when he was three months old, feathered out and able to eat solid food, she went with Pat to fetch Casey home.

It was only a matter of days before Pat was saying to Annie, "I didn't realize I talked so much. Casey's picking up all kinds of words."

"I could have told you," her daughter said with a smile. "Just be sure you watch your language."

"Who, me? I'm a perfect lady."

The sentence Casey learned first was "Where's my glasses?" and coming fast on its heels was "Where's my purse?" Every time Pat began circling the apartment, scanning tabletops, opening drawers and feeling behind pillows, Casey set up a litany: "Where's my glasses? Where's my glasses?"

"You probably know where they are, smarty-pants."

"Where's my purse?"

"I'm looking for my glasses."

"Smarty-pants."

When Pat found her glasses and her purse and went to get her coat out of the closet, Casey switched to "So long. See you later." And when she came home again, after going to the supermarket in the Minnesota weather, she called out, "Hi, Casey!" and Casey greeted her from the den with "Holy smokes, it's cold out there!" She joked, "You took the words right out of my mouth."

"What fun it is to have him," Pat told Annie. "It makes the whole place feel better."

"You know what?" Annie said. "You're beginning to feel better, too."

"So I am. They say laughter's good for you, and Casey gives me four or five great laughs a day."

Like the day a plumber came to repair a leak under the kitchen sink. In his cage in the den, Casey cracked seeds and occasionally eyed the plumber through the open door. Suddenly the parrot broke the silence by reciting, "One potato, two potato, three potato, four…"

"What?" demanded the plumber from under the sink.

Casey mimicked Pat's inflections perfectly. "Don't poo on the rug," he ordered.

The plumber pushed himself out from under the sink and marched into the living room. "If you're going to play games, lady, you can just get yourself another plumber." Pat looked at him blankly. The plumber hesitated. "That was you saying those things, wasn't it?"

Pat began to smile. "What things?"

"'One potato, two potato…'"

"Ah, well, that's not too bad."

"And 'Don't poo on the rug.'"

"Oh, dear, that's bad." Pat got up. "Let me introduce you to Casey."

Casey saw them coming. "Did you do that?" he said in Pat's voice. "What's going on around here?"

The plumber looked from the bird to Pat and back again. "You sure you're not a ventriloquist, ma'am? I thought parrots just squawked and said 'Polly wants a cracker.'"

"Not this parrot."

At that moment Pat sneezed. Casey immediately duplicated the sneeze, added a couple of coughs in imitation of Pat at her allergic worst, finished up with "Wow!" as she often did, then threw in a favorite new phrase he'd picked up when the leak started: "What a mess!" The plumber shook his head slowly, speechlessly, and retired back under the sink.

Casey was so good at imitating Pat that when she telephoned her daughter's house and got one of her grandchildren on the phone, Casey would say, sounding just like her, "Hi. What's going on over there?" It got so that Annie, if she happened to answer the phone, would say, "Hello, Casey. Put Mom on," even when it was Pat herself speaking.

The three grandchildren doted on Casey. Because it amused them vastly, they had learned to belch at will and taught Casey to imitate the sound. The bird would belch loudly and follow it up immediately with "That's gross" in tones of utter disgust. Either that or he'd demand in Pat's voice, "Did you do that?"

When a bout of pneumonia put Pat back in the hospital and Casey stayed at Annie's house, he came home yelling, "Joey, are you up yet? Joey!" Pat remarked to her youngest grandson with some amusement, "Well, I guess I know what goes on at your house in the morning."

In her own house, when Pat woke up in the mornings, she'd hear Casey chittering to himself in his cage in the den. She'd tiptoe to the bathroom, but Casey had acute hearing, and no matter how soundless she'd been, the chittering would stop, there'd be a silence while he listened and then he would call out, "Is the paper here yet?"

Pat usually took the paper and her coffee back to bed. One morning the phone rang. She picked up the extension by her bed and got a dial tone. The next morning it rang again, and although she reached for it promptly, again she got a dial tone. The third morning she realized what it was: Casey had learned to duplicate the ring faultlessly.

Casey ate fruit, vegetables, chicken, egg yolks, pasta and whole-grain breads as well as parrot feed. One day, carrying a piece of melon to him, Pat had it slip from her hands and squash on the floor. "*#@&," she said. Casey eyed her. "Forget you heard that," she ordered hastily. "I didn't say it. I never say it. And I wouldn't have now if I hadn't just mopped the floor." Casey kept his beak shut and Pat relaxed.

Later that day a real estate agent arrived to go over some business papers with her. They were deep in discussion when Casey yelled from the den, "*#@&!"

Both women acted as though they'd heard nothing.

Liking the sibilance, Casey tried it again. "*#@&!" he shouted. "*#@&! *#@&! *#@&! *#@&!"

Pat, caught between humiliation and laughter, put her hand on her guest's arm. "Helen, it's sweet of you to pretend, but we both know you haven't suddenly gone deaf." They broke down in giggles and Casey ordered from the den, "Don't poo on the rug!"

"Oh, you bad bird," Pat scolded after the agent left. "She's going to think I go around all day saying four-letter words."

"What a mess," Casey said.

"You're darned right," Pat told him, reaching into his cage for the cup that hung there.

"How's your water?"

"Oh, dear, don't start saying that now. You really will ruin my reputation."

At work in the kitchen, Pat let Casey out of his cage, where he patrolled the counter and watched for a chance to snatch a lettuce leaf or vegetable peel. He'd sidle to the edge of the counter and drop his prize on the floor, then peek at her and say, "Did you do that?"

His favorite perch in the kitchen was the faucet in the sink; his favorite occupation, trying to remove the washer at the end of it. Once, to tease him, Pat held a handful of water over his head. Casey ceased his attack on the washer and swiveled his head to look at her. "What's the matter with you?" he demanded sharply.

If he disappeared from the kitchen and Pat heard him say, "Oh, you bad bird! You want to go back in your cage?" she knew to come running, that Casey was pecking at either the cane backs of her dining room chairs or the wallpaper in the foyer. In desperation, she had strips of clear plastic installed on the corners in the foyer, but still Casey found fresh places to attack.

"Is it worth it?" her son asked when he came to visit. "The front hall is beginning to look like bomb damage."

"Listen," Pat said, "give me my choice between a perfect, lonely house and a tacky, happy one, and I'll take the tacky one any day.

As a matter of fact, I'd be so devastated to lose Casey that I've been teaching him his phone number in case I ever forget and leave a window or door open."

With a bit of prompting, Casey repeated the number. Pat's son listened solemnly, then advised the bird, "Just be sure you don't fly out of your area code, Casey."

One thing she could do to limit the damage, Pat decided, was to have Casey's claws clipped. On the drive to the vet's office, Casey rode silently in a carrying case beside her on the front seat until they were almost there, when suddenly he had a thought. "Where's my purse?" he demanded.

"What, you forgot your purse, you bad bird?" Pat joked. "You mean, I'm going to have to pay the doctor?"

To trim Casey's claws without getting bitten, the vet wrapped him tightly in a towel, turned him on his back, and handed him to an assistant to hold while he went to work. Helplessly Casey looked over at Pat and repeated a phrase she used when sympathizing with him. "Oh, the poor baby," he said piteously.

Occasions like this make Pat wonder if Casey knows the meaning of the words he's saying. On the whole, she's inclined to believe he simply connects certain phrases with certain actions, but sometimes the words are so apropos that she can't be sure. Recently a guest lingered on and on, standing talking in the doorway, until finally Casey called out impatiently, "Night-night!" When introduced on a different evening to a guest who had spent two hours talking nonstop about himself, Casey looked him up and down and delivered his opinion: "What a mess!"

When Pat wants him to learn something, however, Casey can be maddeningly mum. For her first Christmas back on her feet, Pat invited her children and grandchildren to a family dinner and hatched a scheme of teaching Casey to sing "Jingle Bell Rock." "It'll be your contribution to the festivities," she told him.

"Where's my glasses?"

"Never mind that. Just listen to me." But as often as Pat coached him, singing "Jingle bell, jingle bell, jingle bell rock" as she danced around the kitchen, the bird simply looked at her with a distinct air of wonder at her foolishness and said, "Wow!"

A week before Christmas Pat gave up. "All right, you stubborn creature, forget it. You probably can't carry a tune anyway."

Taking a beakful of seeds, Casey shook his head and flung them in a radius around his cage, cocked his head and listened to them rain on the floor. "Did you do that?" he demanded in Pat's voice. "Shame on you, you bad bird!"

On Christmas day he belched for the grandchildren and said, "That's gross," and once, almost plaintively, he inquired, "What's going on around here?" amid the noise of laughter and packages being ripped open, but all through dinner he was silent. When it was time for dessert, Pat turned the lights down and touched a match to the plum pudding. The brandy blazed up. At that moment, with impeccable timing, Casey burst into "Jingle bell, jingle bell, jingle bell rock!"

With her health so much improved, Pat decided on a three-week European vacation. "You'll be all right," she told Casey. "You can stay with Annie and the kids."

"Phew," said Casey, which was what Annie said when she cleaned the bottom of his cage of the bits of food he'd discarded. "Ouch," he added, which was what he used to scare the family's golden retriever when the dog put his nose too close to the cage.

Annie laughed. "The dog has a lot more trouble with an animal who talks than you have with him," she told Casey.

The day Pat was due back, Annie returned Casey so he'd be there when Pat got out of the taxi from the airport. "Hi, Casey!" Pat called as she unlocked the door. There was no answer from the den. "Holy smokes, it's cold out there!" she shouted. Still no answer. Pat dropped her coat and hurried into the den. Casey glared at her. "Hey, aren't you glad to see me?" The bird moved to the far side of the cage. "Come on, Casey, don't be angry at me," Pat urged. "What do you say, shall we do the dishes?" She opened the door of the cage and held out her hand. Casey dropped to the bottom of the cage and huddled there.

In the morning Pat tried again. And the next day, and the next. Casey refused to speak. But finally, on the fifth day after Pat's return, he consented to climb on her wrist and be carried to the living room. When she sat down in the easy chair, he shifted uneasily and seemed about to fly away. "Please, Casey," Pat said softly. "I know I was away a long time, but you've got to forgive me."

Tentatively Casey took a few steps up her arm. But then he moved back to her knee and revolved uncertainly. "Were you frightened I wasn't ever coming back? Is that it?" Pat asked quietly. "Darling Casey, bonding goes two ways. I belong to you just as much as you belong to me." Casey cocked his head. "I'll never not come back if I can help it."

Step by step, Casey moved up her arm. Slowly Pat crooked her elbow. After a few moments Casey nestled down with his head on her shoulder. Pat stroked his head, smoothing his feathers with her forefinger. Finally Casey spoke.

"I love you, Pat Myers," he said.

Sister Smog and the Windshield Viper

In the Hermitage of Christ the King in Sebastopol, California, Sister Michael of God turned on the radio. She did this once a day to get the news, which she then passed on to the tiny community of contemplative nuns living in solitude, each in her own wooden hut, on ten acres of a tree-covered hillside.

It was the huts Sister Michael was thinking of as she listened. The community had exhausted its resources to pay for the cutting down of some dead trees that were threatening to fall on the huts, and now there was a new threat. Termites were gnawing away at the huts' foundations. Where would the nuns find the $1,000 needed to have the buildings termite-proofed?

The news ended and Sister Michael was reaching for the dial when her ear was caught by an announcement. Station KABL, San

Francisco, in honor of the upcoming St. Patrick's Day, was sponsoring a snake race for charitable organizations. "First prize is two thousand dollars!" the announcer said. Sister Michael snapped to attention. Her eyes rolled heavenward. "Oh, no, Lord, I'm half Irish," she protested. "You can't really expect me to have anything to do with snakes." But just in case He did, she sent for an entry blank.

When the form arrived, Sister Michael reluctantly filled it out. Name of entrant? If she put down "Sister Michael of God," that would really commit her. Yet her initials, S.M.O.G., would look silly. So she compromised: "Sister Smog." Name of snake? *Goodness,* she thought with a snort, *does the snake really have to have a name? Well, in that case…* "Windshield Viper," she wrote.

Sister Michael mailed the form, a safe enough act, she thought, since Sebastopol was fifty miles from San Francisco and she had no way of getting there. But then friends of the Hermitage offered to drive her. On St. Patrick's Day, she prayed all the way to the city for a flat tire, to no avail. They arrived at Crown-Zellerbach Plaza at noon, just as the Irish band struck up. "Snakes alive," muttered Sister Michael, "I'm in for it."

When she confessed to her neighbor in the registration line that she was as nervous as an early Christian martyr on her way into Rome's Colosseum, the man tried to reassure her. "There's only one thing you got to remember," he said. "Don't hold the snake too tight. I did that last year and it turned around and bit me."

"I'll remember," Sister said weakly. She had no intention of holding the snake too tight. Or too loose. Or, for that matter, holding it at all.

At the registration table she was given a wooden dowel ("You can rap the table, Sister, but not the snake"), a piece of cardboard ("In case the snake starts going the wrong way"), a green paper derby ("To get you in the St. Patrick's Day spirit") and instructions to choose a snake from the supply in the green garbage can.

With the derby perched on top of her headgear, Sister Michael edged toward the snake-filled can. Withdrawing a shoe box from under her habit, she held it out to the man in charge. "You know more about snakes than I do," she said ingratiatingly. "Would you choose a fast one and put it in the box for me, please?"

The man calmly reached in and came up with twenty inches of thrashing gopher snake, which he popped into the shoe box. "Hey, what've you got in there?" he said as Sister Michael clapped the lid on.

"A hot water bottle. I heard that snakes like to be warm."

The man hooted. "You'll put him to sleep. Either that or you'll cook him."

The race was to be run in preliminary heats, semifinals and then the final. Every once in a while, as she waited for her heat to be called, Sister gently shook the box. No signs of life came from within. Should she try to peek in? The snake might be coiled, waiting to strike. Should she try to get the hot water bottle out? By now, if he was still alive, the snake probably considered the box his cave and would defend it fiercely.

"In lane number four," the loudspeaker boomed, "Sister Smog racing Windshield Viper!" Laughter, followed by a loud cheer, came from a Catholic Youth Organization gang. Sister waved her derby and advanced to the eighteen-foot-long racing table. Gingerly she snatched the lid from the box and shook Windshield Viper out into lane four.

The snake lay as loosely tangled and motionless as an old piece of rope. Sister Michael tried to see if his eyes were open, but she could locate only his tail, not his head. "Oh, dear, what have I done to you?" she murmured miserably. It was one thing to be afraid of the snake, quite another to have roasted him alive. The announcer's voice came over the loudspeaker: "On your mark…get set!" Hastily Sister drew a vial of holy water from under her habit. "Please be all right. Please don't be dead," she whispered, and sprinkled the holy water on the snake's tail.

Windshield Viper shot into the air like a broken mainspring as the starting gun went off. Was it the cold holy water after the warm hot water bottle? The Viper was halfway to the finish line when he landed. The CYO group cheered wildly.

"Windshield Viper in the lead!" The announcer was calling the race. "Snake Hips coming up fast in lane six! Eve in lane two disqualified for jumping lanes! Here comes Star and Garter in three! There goes Star and Garter in three! Wrong way! Monty Python in lane one still in the starting gate!"

Windshield Viper rose for a look over the partition between lanes. Sister Smog blocked his view with the piece of cardboard. The Viper stuck out his tongue and waggled it at her. Snake Hips passed. Sister banged frantically on the table with her dowel. "Feel the vibes, Viper!" she shouted. "Get moving with the vibes!"

"It's Windshield Viper coming up fast! Windshield Viper takes the lead! And the winner is…Windshield Viper by a length!"

Sister ran around the table. Windshield Viper was sliding off the end. She grabbed him and slid him into the box, on top of the hot water bottle. Her CYO partisans were celebrating the victory. She doffed her derby, blew them a kiss and retired to the sidelines to catch her breath.

Some moments later she said to herself: "Did I do that? Did I really do that? Bare-handed, I picked up a snake?" She sat down heavily.

She tried to remember how the Viper had felt. Not cold, not clammy, not slimy. Dry and clean to the touch. She sniffed her hand; there was just the trace of an autumn smell, of dried leaves. It wasn't at all what she'd expected. In fact, it was rather nice.

Poor thing, she thought. *I probably scared him half to death with the holy water. No wonder he stuck his tongue out at me.* Another thought occurred to her. *Maybe he's as frightened of nuns as I am of snakes. Particularly overweight nuns. Particularly overweight nuns wearing derby hats and called Sister Smog. If he's the Viper to me, I could be the S.S. to him.*

Their semifinal heat was called. Sweeping the lid off the shoe box with a flourish, Sister Smog poured Windshield Viper out on the table. He lay as inert as before. But this time she saw his eye. It was open. It was turquoise!

"On your mark...get set!" Out came the holy water. A dash on his tail and... "It's Windshield Viper off to another flying start!"

"Go, Viper, go!" the CYO group yelled. "Yeah, Smog! Yeah, Viper!"

Sister drummed on the table. The Viper curled and slithered, curled and slithered. Sister screamed encouragement. The Viper pressed on. They were a team; Sister was certain of it. The Viper knew what he had to do, and he did it. Sister ran around the table and caught him at the finish line. The cheers from the CYO group were deafening. They'd won the semifinal heat!

Sister picked the Viper up tenderly. He winked at her with one turquoise eye and tried to curl around her arm. "Now, now," she said, "you did great, but none of that." She caught his tail, straightened him out, admired the design of yellow stripes on his back and the way his basic brown shaded into creamy white on his underside, then popped him back in the shoe box. "You warm up for the finals," she told him, "while I scout the competition."

A snake named Max appeared to be the swiftest in the remaining semifinal races. His handler, Sister noticed, blew on the back of his neck, and with each puff, Max straightened and glided forward. It was legal, it was effective, and she must remember to do it.

It was time for the finals. "In lane five, Sister Smog and Windshield Viper!" Under cover of the cheers, as she slid the Viper out on the starting line, she whispered, "Go, Viper, go." He appeared to be asleep. She leaned closer. His eyes were closed. But his mouth…yes, she was sure of it—his mouth was curled in a smile. She had a feeling he knew they were going to win.

"On your mark!" A dash of the holy water and Windshield Viper was off! But she'd been too eager. He'd jumped the gun. She had to bring him back. He flicked his tongue at her. "I don't blame you. What a dope I am. But please, please, remember the termites."

"On your mark…get set!" This time the Viper wasn't startled by the water. "Go, Viper, go!" Sister screamed. He thought about it. "Go,

Viper, go!" the CYO kids yelled. He curled up. "Go, Viper, go!" He felt Sister's hot breath on his neck, uncoiled and took a long glide forward. She beat on the table. "Catch the vibes!" He slid sideways. Sister huffed and puffed. He darted forward, then stopped to listen to the sound of a distant drumming. "Please, W.V.!" Another long glide. And another. He rose and surveyed the finish line. "Go, Viper, go!"

"They're neck and neck! Max and Windshield Viper! They're coming down the home stretch! It's Max! It's Windshield Viper! It's Max! They're at the finish line! And the winner by a nose is... Max! Second, Windshield Viper. Third..."

Sister went around the table and picked up Windshield Viper. He flicked his tongue at her. "You're right. I deserve it. If I hadn't been so clumsy, you'd have won."

A hand caught her sleeve. "Congratulations, Sister. Come over here. Here they are, folks, Sister Smog and the Windshield Viper! Winner of one thousand dollars!"

"What?"

"Second prize, Sister. You've won a thousand dollars."

"Hey, W.V., did you hear that? Enough for the termites!" A turquoise eye flashed. "Oh, you smart snake, you knew it all the time."

When the TV interview was finished, the CYO kids crowded around Sister Smog. "How did you dare hold the snake?" one girl asked.

"Well, I found out he's like all God's creatures," Sister said. "He likes to be treated warmly."

"Why did you call him Windshield Viper? Weren't you afraid he'd just go side to side?"

"Oh, I never thought of that. Maybe I should have called him Julius Squeezer—he came, he saw, he conquered."

With the $1,000 check safely tucked in her habit, Sister returned Viper to the man who had picked him out. "I don't want anything to happen to him," she said.

"Nothing will. They're all going back to the nature preserve where I caught them."

As she reached into the shoe box, Sister Michael said, "Thanks, Viper, for teaching me about snakes. I promise not to be afraid of them anymore if you promise not to be afraid of nuns in green derby hats."

As Windshield Viper slid into the garbage can, his mouth curved in a smile. Sister Michael of God saw it quite clearly.

A Swan Called Porcelain

The eggs had hatched that morning. Ethel Russell watched from her house through binoculars as the mother swan took the newborn cygnets for a brief swim, then signaled them to follow her back to the nest. The muddy bank was slippery, but the babies straggled up it safely—all except the last. That little one slid helplessly back into the water. Struggling, the cygnet tried again. And slid back again. Through the glasses, Ethel could see the baby's beak open and close as she cheeped for help, but the wind was too strong for the mother swan to hear her cries. She was growing weaker. When she skidded into the water a third time, she stayed there. She was going to die.

Ethel dashed to the garage for her husband's long-handled fishing net and raced to the pond. Duke, the father of the baby swans, came charging toward her, defending the nest. Ethel scooped up the cygnet and ran, dodging those outstretched wings with the sharp "elbows" powerful enough to break a person's leg. When Duke judged her route, he went back to eating eelgrass. Ethel circled, trying to sneak close enough to deposit the baby in the nest. This time Duchess joined Duke on the attack. No one, not even Ethel, who often fed the swans, was allowed near the nest. After one more try, Ethel gave up and carried the little puff of pearly gray back to the house.

She knew it was unfair to imprint a wild creature on humans, but in the circumstances she had no choice, and secretly she was thrilled. Ever since her husband, Frank, had retired and they moved from Ohio to the shores of Chesapeake Bay, she had been fascinated by swans. To see the great white bodies of wild swans surging across the sky, to see the porcelain perfection of pinioned swans floating on neighborhood ponds, was a source of joy to her. Frank, knowing this, had had a pond dug on their property and had bought Duke and Duchess for her. Ethel loved seeing them and longed to know them firsthand. Now it seemed fate was about to grant her wish—if she could keep the baby alive.

She had the little cygnet wrapped in a Turkish towel in her lap when Frank came home. Even before she finished telling Frank the story, he was cradling the pretty creature in his big hands, admiring her bright brown eyes and dark bill and feet. "Ethel," he teased, "I think you've just become a mother." Retorting that, if so, this made him a father, Ethel put Frank to work finding a box and lining it with shredded newspaper. When he had suspended a twenty-five-watt bulb above it for heat and rigged up a water jar and feeding station, they settled the cygnet into it. Already Ethel was imagining her grown, so she had the answer when Frank asked what they should name the swan. "Porcelain," she said. "She will be as beautiful as porcelain."

If Frank and Ethel made odd-looking parents for a swan, Porcey, as they quickly came to call her, didn't seem to notice. She accepted them happily, breaking into cheerful *peep-peep*s at the merest glimpse of either of them and following as close as a feathered shadow when they took her for walks in the yard. The only time she seemed disappointed in them was when they didn't join her in the laundry tub for the twice-a-day swim she loved.

Her attachment to Ethel and Frank quickly raised the question of what to do with Porcey when they took a long-planned trip to Michigan to visit Ethel's parents. On the day they intended to start, Porcey would be just thirty days old. It was Frank who suggested that they take Porcey with them. It was Ethel who insisted on a trial run to see how the swan would react to the car.

Cautiously they settled her between them on the front seat in a hat box lined with disposable diapers. Frank eased the car out of the driveway. Porcey gossiped with Ethel. The car picked up speed. Ethel fed Porcey tufts of grass. She and Frank exchanged a congratulatory look just at the moment Porcey spied a car coming toward them. The cygnet dived for the bottom of the hat box. When next the small creature dared to peek above the rim of the box, another car was coming. She dived again. But finally she grew bolder, and a moment came when she held her ground and, with a graceful sweep of her neck, indicated to the oncoming car that it was to go around them.

So went the trip to Michigan, with Porcey between Ethel and Frank imperiously directing traffic, and eating when they ate, sipping water from a thermos and napping. In late afternoon they stopped at a motel surrounded by lawns, and Ethel went in to register. A sign on the desk decreed No Pets.

"Does that apply to birds?" Ethel asked. The owner, perhaps envisioning a canary in a cage, assured her it was all right to take a bird into the room. Even so, Ethel put the lid on the hat box until they had Porcey safely inside and had filled the bathtub for her swim. The cygnet swam and drank, drank and swam, then ducked her head under and beat the water into great sprays of droplets. Hastily Ethel pulled the shower curtain shut. After this workout, with the bathtub drained and filled with newspapers, Porcey settled down and slept until morning.

She awakened the Russells at daybreak with her chirping. After she'd had another swim, Ethel took her out on the lawn, believing it was too early for anyone else to be up. Suddenly around the corner of the building came the proprietor. He stopped in his tracks at the sight of a woman in a negligee and a swan airing her wings on his lawn. He said not a word, just slowly shook his head as though it falls to the lot of a motel keeper to see the darnedest things.

When the Russells arrived in Michigan, they told Ethel's mother that someone was waiting in the car to meet her. "Oh, dear," she wailed, "wait till I powder my nose."

"Never mind," Frank told her smilingly. "She'll love you just as you are." And Porcey did, enjoying every moment of her stay, including an almost endless stream of visitors as news spread of a handsome, perfectly behaved cygnet who liked to sit in people's laps.

Back home, Frank built an enclosure in the garage for Porcey to spend her nights in, fenced in the yard off the patio and sank a watering trough level with the ground, complete with running water so it would always be fresh. Mornings Porcey greeted Ethel at the garage door and they walked together to the yard. If a leaf, a twig or a scrap of paper was there that had not been there the day before, Porcey stood stock-still until Ethel picked it up.

One evening she refused to enter the garage. "What is it, Porcey?" Ethel asked. "What's the matter?" The swan looked up into her face, then back into the dim depths of the garage. Ethel followed the direction of her gaze but saw nothing. "Show me." Porcey looked into her face again and back at the same spot. Not until it moved did Ethel spot the tiny mouse cowering in a corner.

For her birthday that year, Frank gave Ethel an organ. Her playing left a great deal to be desired, but not as far as Porcey was concerned. At ten o'clock every morning the swan marched across the patio and rapped smartly on the glass door. "Come to listen, have you?" Ethel would say, spreading a piece of plastic for her to sit on, not yet having realized that swans are automatically housebroken, taking care of elimination in the water, not on land. Porcey settled on the plastic, crowding so close that Ethel had to be careful not to kick her as she reached for the pedals.

At one o'clock, following the strict routine she had fashioned for herself, as swans are wont to do, Porcey rapped again on the patio door, this time to be let out for a swim in her pool. Although she could see her siblings playing at the same time over in the pond, Porcey never paid the slightest attention to them. She was far more interested in the big ball she bounced from one end of the pool to the other.

When her swim was over, Porcey undertook the daily scrupulous care of her feathers, preening them, removing broken ones and, with the serrated edge of her beak, carefully cleaning soiled ones. As well as serving as brush and comb, a beak is many things to a swan: spoon, sieve, hammer, weapon and all-purpose tool. It is also the means by which swans express their feelings of fondness. Sometimes, in a rush of affection, Porcey would lean all her weight against Ethel and run her beak in long, stroking caresses up and down her back. "Yes, Porcey," Ethel would say as she stroked the swan's back in turn, "I know you love me, and I love you."

One night at a dinner party Porcey caressed a guest she had taken a particular fancy to, giving him such a turn that he dropped his wineglass. Probably she should not have been at the party at all, but the swan loved company, bobbing her head ceremoniously and making little greeting sounds to each person in turn. When she had made the rounds of the guests, she settled on a red velvet pillow, where, with her glistening white feathers and coral beak, she sat like a snow queen until it came time for her to display her talents.

Ethel had taught her to pluck a blade of grass from her lips, which the swan did so deftly and gently that her beak did not graze Ethel's mouth. Frank built on this ability to enlist the swan's aid in his magic tricks. He fanned a deck of cards and, upon command, Porcey plucked out just one and handed it back to him. If he pretended to drop one of his props, she quickly retrieved it and returned it to him. When he suggested that Porcey whisper a number to him, she stretched her neck to its fullest, stood on tiptoe and made little sounds in his ear, and when he asked her for a hug at the end of his act, she spread her wings and gently enfolded him.

The only people Porcey did not care for were deliverymen. Like all swans, Porcey was strongly territorial, and she had only to catch sight of someone on her property to come charging, wings outspread, talons at the ready. The Russells became resigned to searching the shrubbery at the end of the drive for laundry bundles and UPS parcels hastily flung by rapidly departing drivers.

One employee of Frank's was Porcey's particular enemy. Napping on her cushion one morning, she heard his voice at the front door a flight above. In a flash, she was up the stairs and had driven her beak through the screen door before Ethel could stop her. Only after Frank had dismissed the man for an unrelated cause did they learn that the man had once teased Porcey with an electric prod and she had neither forgiven nor forgotten.

But with Ethel and Frank, of course, because she had been less than twenty-four hours old when she came to live with them, Porcey was nothing but affectionate, well behaved and companionable. While they read or watched television in the evening, she often napped on the floor between them, and when she considered it her bedtime, she went and stood by the patio door. They'd let her out, and the three of them would walk together across the lawn to the garage.

In the spring of her second year, on a night of a full moon, Porcey moved from their side. She stopped at the edge of the lawn, lifted her head to the sky and called. "She's calling for a mate," Frank said. "It's time for her to leave us."

"Oh, Frank, how can we let her go?" Ethel cried. But just as parents know that however much they love their children, they must free them to live lives of their own, so Ethel knew that Frank was right. Swans have a life span of twenty to thirty years, and Porcey deserved to have in those decades the dear companionship that she and Frank shared.

The next afternoon Ethel led Porcey to the pond, and the swan glided along behind her as she rowed to a cove at the far end and set up a feeding station there. "Stay, Porcey, stay," Ethel told her, and as though she understood she was on her own now, the swan began a probing exploration of the shores of her cove. Ethel hoped that gradually the other swans would accept Porcey and let her join them, but day after day they drove her away. It became apparent that if Porcey was to have a mate, Frank and Ethel would have to find him for her.

An ad in a game magazine brought word of a fine two-year-old in Cleveland. The Russells made arrangements for him to be shipped, and when they brought him home from the airport, Porcey welcomed him excitedly to her cove. Watching them play and splash together, Frank and Ethel felt rather like parents of the bride.

Alas, they had congratulated themselves too soon. Within a day Porcey was rudely driving the newcomer from the water. When it became evident that this was no passing tiff, the Russells tried again with a bird from Indiana. Purposely they made their visits to the cove less frequent, thinking it might be jealousy that made Porcey difficult. Again all was well at first, but on the fourth day they found Indiana sitting gloomily on the bank while Porcey patrolled her domain triumphantly. Obviously this suitor had been rejected, too.

When the birdman came to pinion that season's offspring of Duke and Duchess (a simple and bloodless procedure if done early, pinioning is the removal of the second joint of one wing to prevent the bird from flying), Ethel and Frank told him of their sad failure as matchmakers. Mr. Miller excused himself. When he returned, he was apologetic. "It's my fault, not Porcey's," he said. Since it takes an expert to tell a male swan from a female, he had sexed Porcey at six months of age and confirmed the Russells' supposition that the cygnet was a female. "Not so," he now said. "She is a he."

A phone call to a breeder in Rhode Island turned up a four-year-old female who had lost her mate. Because swans mate for life, this time it would be a question not only of whether Porcey would accept the newcomer but also of whether the newcomer would accept a new mate. Only because she was young did it seem worth a try. Again Ethel and Frank drove the eighty miles to the airport to meet a plane with a crated swan aboard.

It was dark when they got back home and released the lovely, quiet bird into the water. Soon she was out of sight, but Frank and Ethel lingered by the pond's edge, his arm around her waist, her head resting on his shoulder. The night was warm, the breeze was soft and moonlight made a shimmering path the length of the pond.

Frank's grasp tightened. "Look," he whispered. Into the moonlight glided the two silver swans, as beautiful as porcelain on a mirrored lake. The breeze swung them gently toward each other. As they touched, Porcey lightly ran his beak up and down the newcomer's neck. A moment later the female returned his caress.

Ethel thinks of it often—that moment, that night. Now that Frank is gone, she looks at Porcey and remembers how happy she and Frank were, and she is glad for Porcey that he has found that sweet closeness she and Frank shared. She asks for the little cygnet grown into a swan only that he will be able to keep it as long and lovingly as they did.

An Experiment in Love

The dog discovered them, four newborn kittens abandoned in tall grass beside the road. When Livy returned from her walk carrying the tiny creatures in the palm of her hand, Steve, her husband, ordered, "Get those mice out of here." He was equally adamant when Livy showed him they were kittens. "No more animals," he said firmly. Steve had already been saddled with Livy's dog and three cats, and he was not used to a houseful of pets.

"I won't keep them," Livy promised. "Just until they're old enough to be on their own." Steve looked dubious. "Word of honor," Livy assured him, never dreaming how much she would come to regret that promise.

She made a warm nest for the babies by ripping up an old blue blanket and lining a wicker basket with it. Then she went to a nearby pet store to get advice about feeding them. "You can't raise kittens that young," the storekeeper warned her, but Livy decided to buy a set of toy nursing bottles for dolls and try. She warmed milk and she and the kittens struggled through several false starts until the kittens got the hang of it and drank avidly.

Two hours later they woke and set up an insistent chorus of soft little cries to be fed again. And every two hours after that. Four times in the night Livy crawled out of bed to warm their milk, and in the morning she congratulated herself that they were looking just a little bit stronger, a little bit bigger.

But by afternoon her pleasure had turned to pessimism. The kittens' intake was fine, but there was no outgo. Their little bellies were stretched tight as drums. Livy called everyone she could think of who might know what to do, but nobody had a suggestion. Hanging up after the last fruitless inquiry, she looked at the kittens sadly. So the storekeeper was right after all: she was not going to be able to save them. She picked up one of the kittens and began to rub its taut tummy in commiseration. Suddenly her hand was drenched. She picked up another kitten and rubbed its tummy. The same thing happened. Did a mother cat, after her kittens had nursed, give them a good rough washing? From then on, so did Livy, and the kittens thrived.

Steve, reporting on their progress to the people in his office, came home one evening with word that his secretary had offered to adopt Peaches, Livy's favorite because of her lovely soft coloring. As though it were Peaches's fault that she would soon be leaving her, Livy found herself picking up Peaches less often and making her wait her turn for the bottle instead of feeding her first. Idly she wondered if it would affect Peaches's personality no longer to be treated as special. Then the thought turned itself around. Suppose she gave one of the kittens extra amounts of mothering? Suppose she held and cuddled and talked to it more? Would it grow up to be any different from its siblings? She decided it would be an interesting experiment.

She chose the most unpromising of the kittens as her subject. This was a little black one Steve called Bat Cat because he was so homely with his dull fur, squashed porcine face and little folded flaps of skin for ears. The runt of the litter, Bat Cat was always on the bottom of the kitten heap, the last to be picked up, the last to be fed, the one who got the least attention.

Livy gave the tiny creature a new name—Boston, short for Boston Blackie—and repeated it softly over and over while she held him for his bottle. If he still seemed hungry after he finished one bottle, she gave him a second, and a third, as much as he wanted until, blissfully full, he fell asleep. Then she tucked him into her sweater so that he slept against her beating heart while she worked at her desk. When he woke, she snuffled his small body with her warm breath and talked to him before putting him back in the basket to play with his siblings.

The effect on the kitten was immediate. His newly opened eyes, which, like the others', had been vague and unfocused, became alert, and he studied Livy's face with interest. Quickly he learned his name, and when Livy spoke it, he clambered over the folds of the blue blanket as fast as his unsteady little legs could carry him to her. Now when he was in the sleeping heap of kittens, no longer did he passively accept the bottom spot; sweetly but determinedly he wriggled out from under and nested himself on top. Was it that, sensing himself valued, Boston began to value himself?

He was the first of the kittens to discover he could purr, the first to make endearingly clumsy attempts to wash himself, the first to undertake the adventure of climbing out of the wicker basket. When the others, exhausted from their tumbling play, fell asleep, he climbed over the side of the basket and searched for Livy. Finding her, he struggled to sit up on his haunches and held out his front paws in a plea to be picked up. Unable to resist, Livy lifted the tiny body gently, turned him on his back and nuzzled the star-shaped sprinkling of white hairs on his tummy. After a moment his small paws reached up to pat her cheek and his bright eyes searched hers as he listened to the words she murmured.

Even Boston's looks changed. His fur, from being rusty and rough, grew sleek and shiny. At first the luster was just on his head, but gradually the glossiness moved down his entire body until little Boston gleamed from the tip of his nose to the tip of his tail. Though never beautiful, he became so alert and merry, so trusting and affectionate, that the mere sight of him was a delight. Obviously Livy's experiment in love was an unqualified success, except for one large drawback: in giving Boston so much love, Livy had come to care deeply about him in return.

Secretly she hoped Steve would also be captured by Boston's charm. While he did agree that the extra attention given Boston had had a fascinating effect, Steve's interest was mainly academic. And, unfortunately, Boston was not always tactful. If Steve picked him up, his head swiveled to look for Livy.

As he grew, Boston became ever more responsive, watching until he learned the meaning of each move Livy made. Did she think of starting dinner? He was on his way to the kitchen. Did she think of going outside? He was at the door. One day he made a throaty sound midway between a purr and a miaow. "Yes, little Boss," Livy responded, "I know you're there," and from then on he quickly learned to produce the sound at will. With Livy offering interpretations, such as "Yes, I expect you do want your supper now," and "I'm glad to see you, too, Boss," he added more sounds, specific sounds that meant "supper" and "hello" and "how are you?" until he had a vocabulary of more than thirty "words."

Livy never walked in a room without his volunteering, "Hello." She never said, "How are you, little Boss?" without him answering. In fact, as long as she would talk to him, he would reply, which caused a problem when Livy was on the telephone. Since no one else was present, Boston assumed the words were meant for him and answered so enthusiastically that often Livy had trouble carrying on the human conversation.

After dinner, Boston liked to sit on Livy's shoulder and watch the soap bubbles pop while she washed the dishes. He was in his usual spot one evening when Steve walked in and heard the two of them "talking." "You're going to miss him when he goes," Steve said.

Livy wheeled from the sink. "Oh, Steve..."

Steve looked steadily back. Livy saw from his expression that this was a test between them. Would she keep her word to him or did she value a little black kitten more than his wishes? Steve had had trouble learning to trust, and Livy realized she dare not jeopardize the confidence she had worked so hard to gain. "Yes," she said as evenly as she could. "Yes, I am going to miss him."

Peaches and the ginger-colored cat went to new homes, and soon after their departure, Steve came home with word that someone in his office had recently lost a cat and might be willing to adopt both Boston and Striper. She was coming to inspect the kittens that night. When the doorbell rang, Livy snatched up one of the adult cats, a magnificent tortoiseshell Persian, arranged her among the cushions on the couch and provided a pinch of catnip to keep her there. The woman thought the kittens were cute, but her eyes kept straying to the Persian. She left saying she wouldn't decide just now about the kittens, not until she'd looked into the possibility of getting a purebred.

But Livy had no countermove when Steve came home with word of a church bazaar that was requesting kittens to be donated for sale at a pet table. It was obvious that these were to be Livy's last days with Boston. Now when she cradled him in her arms, it was often tears on her cheeks that he patted. "Oh, little Boss, it's going to be so empty without you," she would tell him, and his eyes would narrow with the effort to understand her distress.

The day before Boston and Striper were to go to the fair, a friend of Steve's secretary said she would like one of the kittens for her six-year-old son and they would come that evening to choose between Boston and Striper. Livy's heart contracted when the little boy, looking like a miniature football player, stormed through the door. How could such a tiny creature as Boston survive the roughness of his hands in play? Marching up to the kittens, the boy grabbed his choice around the stomach with both hands and announced, "His name is Grady and he's mine." He had chosen Striper.

So Boston would go alone to the church fair. Steve called at noon the next day to remind Livy that a description of his age, sex and food preferences was to go with him. "I've already typed it up," Livy said. Wary that she might have worded it in such a way that no one would want Boston, Steve asked her to read it to him. It included this final note: "Boston has been hand-raised with an unusual amount of loving attention, which has made him extraordinarily intelligent and responsive. He is gentle, perfectly behaved, loves all games, likes to ride in the car, has a large vocabulary and is a devoted companion. Please treat him with the great affection he will give you."

Steve was silent for a moment. "You've made him sound like an exceptional creature," he said.

"He is," Livy said, and hung up.

She was in the kitchen getting dinner that night when Steve came home. Boston went to the door to greet him, but Livy couldn't; she was fighting too hard not to cry. There was a long delay before Steve joined her. When he did, he was carrying Boston, who had a big red ribbon tied around his neck. Silently Steve held out an envelope. Inside was a Christmas card, and written on it was: "It's only November, but let's give ourselves a Christmas present."

"If you can be big enough to let him go," Steve said with love and understanding in his eyes, "I can be big enough to let him stay."

Livy reached out to hug Steve through her happy tears, and Boston, wriggling to get to her, slipped through Steve's hands. As the kitten struck the floor, he screamed terribly. One of his hind legs stuck out at an angle. Thinking he had dislocated his hip, Livy gave the leg a sharp yank. Boston screamed again, tried to run and collapsed.

His leg was broken, but the vet had even sadder news for them. Boston was suffering from an inborn defect in calcium absorption. Kittens with this problem could sometimes be saved by injections of calcium, and if they survived to adulthood, the condition tended to correct itself. But there was no guarantee the treatment would work and the cost of the injections would mount up. Did they want to have him put down instead?

Quickly Livy said, "I'll pay for the injections."

"Nonsense," said Steve. "He's our cat." And he told the vet to do what he could to save Boston.

The vet marveled at little Boston's disposition. Even though Bossie knew he was in the office for his daily injection, he greeted the doctor cheerfully and crept into Livy's arms to be comforted only when the ordeal was over. His leg healed quickly, although he walked with a funny little swing of his hip, but three weeks after the last injection, he took a tumble and it was obvious the other hind leg was broken. This time the vet did not even ask if he should try to save him. Ten more injections and Boston was racing around as nimbly as ever, the stiff-legged swing of his rump even more pronounced but not handicapping. Little Boston's calcium deficiency made him a very expensive Christmas present, but he was over it.

It is said that when a child is born into the world, the first years of his or her life are taken up with finding answers to the most basic of questions: "Is it a good and benign world? Can the people in it be trusted? Am I loved?" If a little kitten can also be curious about such things, the special love given Boston answered all his questions with a resounding yes.

It showed in his favorite activity, which was to fly across the back lawn, leap at a tree and scramble ten or fifteen feet up it. Then he would call. Livy would answer, and he would call again until Livy spotted his tiny body clinging to a branch. "What's the matter, Boss?" she would say. "Can't you get down?" He would admit he couldn't. The first time it happened, Steve went for a ladder while Livy stood under the tree, arms outstretched to catch the teetering cat. He did fall, and Livy caught him. But had he fallen or jumped? Livy wasn't sure. The next time he was stuck, Livy held out her arms and said, "Jump, Boss," and he did, instantly, with absolute confidence, right into her arms. And every time after that.

On the first warm day of summer that year, Livy put her kayak in the river that bordered their land and paddled upstream. Boston followed worriedly along the bank, calling to her, and when he came to an opening in the underbrush, he scrambled down the bank and out on a rock. There he stood, his front paws in the water, his whole body leaning so yearningly forward that Livy was afraid he was going to launch himself into the stream. She steered the kayak in beside him, picked him up and put him in her lap. He sat pressed against her, his eyes wide, an occasional involuntary shudder running through him, while she paddled upstream and then turned the kayak and drifted down on the current. Boston did not move or make a sound. The current carried them in toward the bank. They were still six feet away from it when, without warning, Boston catapulted himself in a black streaking arc from boat to shore, landing without a fraction of an inch to spare. His calculation of the distance he could jump had been exact. Then he turned and spoke anxiously to Livy until she, too, was safely back on dry land.

Another time she heard worry in his voice was early one morning when she was awakened by his talking through the crack under the bedroom door. At first she told him to go back to sleep, that it was not yet breakfast time, but he spoke so insistently that she got up to see what was troubling him. Instead of rushing into the room to leap on the bed for his morning loving, he turned and hurried halfway downstairs, then stopped to look back at Livy and spoke again. Verifying at each step that Livy was following, he led her downstairs and into the living room. As she entered, there was a whirring sound and the three older cats flashed to the top of the couch. They were in pursuit of a starling that had come down the chimney in the night. Livy shouted, distracting the cats. The bird flew to the top of the curtain—and finally out of one of the windows Livy opened.

Although Boston also saved another bird's life in the same way—by coming to fetch her in the garden and leading her to where a blue jay was immobilized by a stick wedged in its beak—Boston was not the nonhunter these incidents would suggest. He loved to stalk flies and wasps, instinctively knowing that the one could be swatted with impunity but the other only with lightning-fast caution, and the Persian introduced him to the excitement of mouse hunting. She cornered one in the cellar one day and allowed Boston to share in its capture. The next thing Livy knew, he was vomiting violently and up came the remains of the mouse.

Having observed that, Livy was not concerned when, on an evening in July, she went out to pick lettuce in the back garden and found Boston crouched over the remains of a rabbit. "Good heavens, Bossie," she said, "however did you catch that?" He looked at her, glassy-eyed from overeating, his stomach round as a barrel, and she assumed that the rabbit, like the mouse, would soon be coming up. But it stayed down and the next morning Boston was back to normal size.

A few days later he began to seem listless. Livy felt his ears and they were cool, his nose and it was moist, and decided that it was only some minor indisposition. But the next afternoon when he did not greet Livy at the door and she found him sitting hunched in a corner, she gathered him up and set out for the vet's. On the way there she remembered the rabbit. Boston was too small to catch a healthy rabbit. Perhaps it had already been dead when he found it. A nearby railroad had recently sprayed a defoliant....

The vet scolded Livy for assuming that a cat's nose and ears are reliable indicators of his health. Boston had a fever of 105 degrees and was severely dehydrated. What was needed was to get as much food and medicine into him as possible. Livy stopped at a supermarket to get the liver, baby food and milk the vet had suggested and an eyedropper to feed him with if he did not eat voluntarily. Back home, she went around to the passenger side of the car and lifted him in her arms. He cried out, stiffened, his spine arched and it was over. Little Boston was dead.

Livy could not believe it. For eleven months she and Boston had been so close. They had talked so clearly. How could she not have known he was so ill? Steve tried to comfort her, but his own eyes were clouded with tears as they buried the tiny black body, now featherlight, under the tree he had loved to jump from. When the last trowelful of dirt was in place and they had transplanted myrtle to cover his grave, Steve stood looking down at the spot where Boston lay. Finally he said, "You were right. He was a truly remarkable small creature."

Months later, when the ache of missing Boston had eased enough to let Livy think back on her experiment, she decided to visit the other kittens, now grown. Peaches was sweet and bland. Ginger was sharp and unfriendly. Striper spent most of his time hiding under furniture. Only Boston had been unique in his intelligence and affectionate, outgoing nature. That love has unmatched power to nurture, to bless, to make cheerful and whole, Livy's experiment had demonstrated. But it was little Boston who proved that when you give love freely, you get something quite extraordinary in return.

Goose Steps

"You've got a sick goose over there," Gene Fleming remarked to his sister-in-law as they walked toward his car. He had stopped by Billee Schuck's farm in Harvard, Nebraska, to pick up some ducklings for his pond and noticed a goose who kept toppling over.

Billee didn't even look around. "Naw, that's Andy," she said. "He was born without feet."

With the ducklings stowed in his pickup, Fleming went over to take a look at the handicapped goose. "You're a gutsy fella," he said as Andy, his wings flapping wildly, tried to run away. The gray goose looked like a little boy on his first pair of stilts. His legs, thin as twigs, ended in callused knobs the size of silver dollars. The only way Andy could stay upright was to run as fast as he could until his momentum pitched him forward on his breast. He fell now, and Gene reached out to smooth his feathers. Because geese tend to be peevish creatures, Gene expected to get his hand sharply nipped, but Andy was quiet under his touch.

Gene kept thinking about the crippled goose as he headed home to his own ninety-one-acre spread in Hastings. Had there been an appeal in those shoe-button eyes as Andy lay forlornly on the ground, his breast caked with mud? Gene thought about how he was a Shriner and Shriners are dedicated to helping crippled children. "That goose is just as helpless as a little child," he told himself. "I ought to be able to do something for him."

He put his inventive mind to work, just as he had years before on another occasion. That time his sympathy had gone out to cows tormented by insect bites, and he set about inventing a device they could rub against to scratch themselves and get a dose of insecticide and soothing oil on the itching spot. He called it the Rol-Oyl Cattle Oiler, and his company, the Fleming Manufacturing Co. of Hastings, Nebraska, had by that time made and sold more than four hundred thousand of them.

As soon as he got back to Hastings, Gene called his sister-in-law. "Billee," he said, "how about I take that footless goose off your hands? He'll be better off swimming in my pond than tryin' to walk on those sticks of his."

Billee Schuck refused. "I'm saving him for Thanksgiving dinner," she said. "Besides, even though he can't mate because he can't stand up, Polly is his wife and I'm not going to separate them."

"I'll take Polly, too," Gene proposed. Still his sister-in-law said no. Finally Gene offered to trade two blue-eyed Pomeranian geese for them. Telling him he was crazy to trade valuable geese for a gray one without feet, Billee accepted the offer.

Gene fetched Andy and Polly and turned them loose in his pond.

Polly sailed gracefully off. Andy, struggling to follow her, worked his footless stilts as fast as an eggbeater but succeeded only in churning up silt. Gene lifted him out of the pond. "Okay, young fella," he said, "let's see what we can figure out for you."

Gene had his back to the pond while he was examining Andy's stilts and didn't see Polly climb out. She rushed at him and grabbed his pants, tugging furiously. "It's okay, Polly. I'm gonna help him if I can," Gene assured her. But Polly was determined to defend Andy. "Exile for you, my girl," Gene decreed. "You're gonna have to stay out of the way until I get your old man on his feet." He knew from Billee Schuck that Polly had spent weeks the previous spring sitting on eggs that never hatched and had finally taken to mothering a clutch of ducklings. "Just you be patient," he told her as he shooed her into a shed. "With a little bit of luck, I'll fix you up a proper husband."

Shoes, Gene decided. Andy needed some sort of shoes. Gene went into town and bought a pair of white leather baby shoes, size zero. Andy was deceptively patient while Gene slipped them over his knobs, laced them and tied a bow. Then the goose leaned over, untied the bows with his beak and pulled his legs free. Gene got some glue and glued the bows to the shoes. Andy fell into the pond, kicked one shoe off and, paddling with the other, swam in a circle until Gene caught him.

Bit by bit, experimenting as he went, Gene worked out what was needed. On his left foot Andy had a bit of a heel, but there was none on his right foot, and his right leg was cocked. Gene placed sponge rubber toward the outside of the right shoe and at the top of the shoe on the left side so that both soles would rest flat on the ground.

More sponge rubber went in the toes of the shoes. He cut the back of the right shoe so the cocked leg would fit in and punched small holes into the soles so that water would drain out.

In the meantime Andy's life was being made miserable by two Chinese white geese who considered it their job to patrol the farmyard. Their hearing was acute and their honks so loud that they scared away coyotes, raccoons and possums wishing to dine on duckling, but they also felt that a goose who could not strut was an interloper and attacked Andy, pecking at his legs and wings and sending him cowering into corners. "Never mind, Andy," Gene told him. "One of these days you'll show 'em."

When the shoes were ready, Gene drew little white socks over Andy's knobs, laced the greatly adapted shoes snugly around his ankles and glued the bows. He set Andy on his feet. The goose sank to the ground helplessly. He seemed to think he had mud on his legs, and for three days kicked backward trying to shake the shoes off. Unable to rid himself of them, he lay on his breast and pushed himself along the ground with the tips of the shoes. Gene debated getting him a skateboard, but he decided first to have a go at trying to teach Andy to walk.

He buckled a dog harness around the goose's body and dangled him from a leash like a puppet on a string. "You've got toes now, Andy. Lean into them and take a step." Over and over he bounced Andy on his new feet. "Come on, Andy, you can walk if you think you can. All it takes is believing you can."

Three hours went by. Still Gene was patient. "You can do it, Andy. I know you can." Suddenly Andy took a baby step. It wasn't more than four inches, but it was a step. "That's it, Andy!" Gene exulted. "You've got it. Do it again. Lean into your toes. And again. Good boy! You're walking!"

Staggering like a fat baby in diapers, Andy inched around the farmyard. Gene unhooked the leash. Andy teetered but stayed upright. He looked at Gene. "You've done it," Gene congratulated him, and as though he understood, Andy stretched his neck and, lifting his head high, honked exultantly. He was six inches taller than he had ever been before.

Because he never had reason to use them, Andy's ankles were stiff and his walk tended to resemble a drunken stagger. But he stayed on his feet, and after several days of practice he was strutting around the farmyard. Gene released Polly from the shed to come and look at her mate. She stalked directly to Andy and stared at his new white feet. "What do you think, Polly?" Gene asked her.

She gave a shake of her head and flounced away as if to say, *He's a silly goose.* Suddenly there was a terrific honking. The two Chinese whites were bearing down on Polly and Andy. With a flurry of feathers, Polly fled into the pond, but Andy stood his ground. Rising on the toes of his new shoes, he beat the air with his wings and intimidated the Chinese geese into retreat. Then he marched to the pond and launched himself into the water. With his legs stretched out behind him, kicking his "feet" in unison, Andy propelled himself forward like a paddle-wheel steamer. Quickly he outdistanced Polly, then turned and proudly swam circles around her.

The principle of the shoes was a success, but the shoes themselves were worn out in a month. Since they cost $12.99 a pair and the life expectancy of a goose is thirty years, Gene figured it would cost him close to $5,000 to keep Andy on his feet unless he could come up with a substitute. He went to town again and this time returned with a pair of Nike sneakers. They worked perfectly and proved much more durable.

Word got around Hastings that Gene Fleming was buying baby shoes for a goose. The local paper carried a picture of Andy standing tall in his sneakers, and a teacher asked Gene if he would bring Andy to school to show the children. "Unless," she said, knowing the temperament of geese, "you think he'll snap at them."

"Not Andy," Gene said confidently. "He likes people." Gene set about fashioning a carrier in which Andy could travel comfortably with his head out, bought him a new red harness and leash, made a tape recording of Polly honking and off they went to the school.

Andy strutted back and forth in front of the class, showing off how well he could walk, and when Gene played the tape of Polly's voice, he lifted his head and honked joyously. The children loved it, and Andy did not mind at all when they crowded around and petted him.

The visit was such a success that Gene took Andy to every grammar school in Hastings and began answering requests from neighboring towns. "We don't often get a chance to do something really big for our fellow creatures, human or animal," Gene told the children. "But keep your eyes open for the little things you can do, because sometimes little things can make an awfully big difference. Like the difference shoes have made for Andy."

The letters Gene gets from the children after Andy visits suggest they understand. "If I find anything that's hurt," one little boy wrote,

"I'll try to fix him like you fixed Andy." But Gene cherishes most a February card from a girl in the second grade. "Andy's my valentine," she printed on a big red heart. "But I love Mr. Fleming because he gave Andy goose steps."

"It's a funny thing how blessings come in disguise, isn't it, Andy?" Gene sometimes muses as he drives home with the goose on the seat beside him. "What seems like the worst thing that could've happened, like your being born without feet, turns out to be the best. What other goose gets to wear sneakers and go to school and be made an honorary member of the chamber of commerce and have the Eagles give him a birthday party?" He reaches out to smooth Andy's feathers where the carrier has ruffled them, and Andy gently catches Gene's sleeve in his beak to give it a tweak. Is that a wink or a blink of Andy's shoe-button eyes? Gene is never quite sure, but just in case, he always winks back.

The Dog Who Healed a Family

What led up to the catastrophe was this. The Dykhouse family was watching a cable TV show about hard-to-adopt children, and a little boy with a crooked Jimmy Stewart grin limped into their affections. "Why couldn't we take him?" proposed eleven-year-old Julee Dykhouse.

"Hey, yeah, that'd be cool," Steve, fourteen, agreed. "I'd have a guy to play with."

"It'd be like bookends," Sherry, who was a serious thirteen, said. She was referring to the fact that Steve had been adopted as a baby, and if a younger boy was added to the family, he and Steve would flank the two natural daughters. "What do you think, Mom? Dad?"

Sharon and Don Dykhouse had been pretending to read the newspaper, but they, too, had felt the tug of the little boy. They looked at each other. In their fieldstone house there was enough room. In their ninety acres of Wisconsin fields and woods there was enough room. In their hearts there was enough room. The next day Sharon traveled to the city and the adoption agency. But in the delay between the taping of the TV show and its airing, the lame boy had already gone to a family.

So that was the end of that generous idea. Except that some weeks later a photo of another eight-year-old boy arrived from the agency. *Yes,* thought Sharon, responding to the vulnerability the lad was trying to disguise by the straightness of his slight body and the protective way his arms sheltered two little girls, one on either side of him. Even when she read the letter that came with the picture and learned the girls were his sisters and the adoption agency stipulated that the three children must be kept together, Sharon still thought, *Yes.*

"If you can manage three more, so can I," was Don's cheerful response to the snapshot. His veterinary practice was large enough to support them.

He and Sharon looked at the letter from the agency again. Timothy, eight, Claire, five, and Laurie, four, they read, were the children of a college graduate who had emerged from a severe automobile accident with her looks intact but with her brain so damaged that right and wrong were no longer meaningful to her and she went with any man who paid for drinks and supplied drugs. Thus the children had unknown fathers and an unpredictable, frequently forgetful mother. When she disappeared for days, Timothy took care of the little girls as best he could, feeding them whatever he could find in the house, washing and dressing them, and when his mother brought a strange man home, he tried to protect the crying baby from being hit—or worse.

The day their mother forgot them on a street corner in five-degree weather was the day the child welfare authorities discovered their situation and began checking on them. When they visited and found the girls covered with bruises, they placed the children in foster homes. But the youngsters were so unhappy at being separated—and so difficult to handle in their unhappiness—that now the agency was seeking an adoptive home for the three together.

Sharon and Don held a family conference with Steve, Sherry and Julee. Again Sherry commented on the symmetry: a boy and two girls, just like they were. Feeling good about the decision, all agreed that Tim and Claire and Laurie should come to them.

It was a disaster.

Timothy, at eight, was a little old man who had never learned to play. Weighted down with responsibility, he was cautious, rigid, pessimistic and humorless. When Steve tried to teach him to throw a ball, he displayed the aptitude and interest of a wooden Indian, and when the girls tried to engage him in games of tag, he tripped over his own feet and scurried back inside the house. The Dykhouse children quickly concluded he was about as much fun to have around as an undertaker.

Claire, on the other hand, never stopped smiling. The smile was as bland and unvarying as though it were painted on a doll, and she smiled it no matter what was said or done to her. The only thing she was absolutely positive about was that her favorite color was black, and she spent much of her time jabbing a black crayon into scraps of paper and secreting the scraps around the house. She alternated this behavior with hitting herself on the nose until the blood flowed in twin rivers and then smearing the blood on the walls.

One afternoon when Sharon Dykhouse tried to head off this behavior by proposing a doll's tea party with the blue luster cups her daughters loved, four-year-old Laurie had a temper tantrum and upended the table. Laurie's temper tantrums came four and five times a day. Often, during them, she flew at her sister and raked Claire's face with her fingernails, and one terrible day she stabbed her with the pointed end of a compass. Sharon pleaded with Claire to defend herself, at least until Sharon could come to her aid, but Claire only smiled her bland smile.

Every evening when Don came home, Laurie suffered a panic attack, screaming and weeping for minutes at a time. She was terrified of men and would not let Don come near her, nor would she allow Sharon to comfort her; she went rigid at any attempt to touch her, however gently.

Peace and comity leaked out of the house like air from a punctured tire. The old and new threesomes of children shunned each other, and the older children became progressively more alienated even from their parents because of the presence of this difficult trio. Sharon sought professional help. She took the new children for diagnosis and treatment, engaged in play therapy with them at home and tried, sometimes forcibly, to make them let her cuddle them. But the children could not trust, nor relax, nor believe their world had become better and kinder in any meaningful way.

One day when open warfare had erupted and Sharon felt she was at the end of her rope and ready to be hung from it, the telephone rang. It was Don calling from his office. "Put the kids in the car and come on down."

"What for?"

"You'll see," Don said, and hung up.

Sharon's voice was so irritable as she ordered the kids into the car that none dared object. So it was that all six children stormed into the veterinary clinic's waiting room, alarming a large, black, silky-haired dog who leaped to her feet and erupted into deep-chested barks in defense of her owners and their baby.

Alerted by the noise, Don emerged from his examining room. "These people are moving to the city," he told Sharon, introducing her to the young couple. "Their dog is a good watchdog and loves children, but they can't have her in the city and they can't find anyone to take her, so they've brought her here to be put down."

"Oh, no!" Julee, an even more passionate animal lover than her parents, protested. "Daddy, you can't! Mom, can't we take her?"

Sharon bit her lip so she wouldn't comment about the trouble they were in because of the last time Julee had proposed an adoption. She glared at Don for putting her on the spot in front of the children and the young couple.

"She's only a year old, and a strong, healthy dog," Don said, defending himself. "But it's up to you."

Rage flooded Sharon. Sure, Don wanted the dog because her silky fur was like Rusty's, the favorite companion of his teenage years. And sure, he'd known that Julee would fall in love with the dog because she looked like Blackie, their Labrador who had been stolen months before. But why hadn't he given some thought to her position? She was desperately trying to hold this family together, and the last thing she needed was one more frightened and displaced creature to contend with.

"Keep her in the kennel and we'll see," Sharon ground out between stiff lips, and marched the children back out to the car.

Driving home, Sharon waited for the pleas to start. Not from the little kids—they were afraid of dogs, just as they were afraid of everything else. But even Julee said nothing. Suddenly Sharon realized what her children were thinking: she would have said yes to the dog if it hadn't been for the newcomers, so now the Dykhouse children had one more reason to resent the little kids. When they arrived home, Sharon called Don and said to bring the dog home, that they would try her out.

"What's her name?" she asked before she hung up.

"Shaneen."

"If she's as dumb as her name, she's not staying."

That night, all night long, untempted by the blanket she could have curled up on inside the snug doghouse, Shaneen stretched to the length of her chain and howled. In the morning Julee said numbly, "We can't keep her, I guess."

"Go bring her in," Sharon said. "Let's see if that stops her barking."

The dog huddled in a corner of the kitchen while the children raced to get ready for school. When all were gone except Laurie, Sharon knelt and looked across the room at Shaneen.

"Come here," she said.

The dog wagged the tip of her tail timidly and promptly wet the floor.

"Bad dog! Bad dog!" Laurie screamed. "Go away!"

Sharon caught the child's upraised arm before she could strike the dog. "Not bad," Sharon corrected quietly. "Frightened. She doesn't know us. She doesn't know if we'll be kind to her." She sat on the floor and spoke quietly. "Shaneen...Shaneen, it's all right. This is your home now. We'll never hurt you. We'll love you and take care of you. You'll be all right, I promise you."

The dog bellied across the vinyl tiles until she was close enough to sniff Sharon's hand. As Laurie looked on, Shaneen sighed thankfully and laid her head in Sharon's lap. Laurie reached out and touched her. The dog's tail thumped lightly. Sharon held her breath. Had Laurie known the message was for her, too? Laurie buried her face in Shaneen's silky ruff, and Sharon shifted her arm to enfold the child as well as the dog. The child didn't pull away. It was the first bit of contact she had allowed.

Later that day Laurie had a temper tantrum and threw herself on the floor kicking and screaming. Shaneen looked on from a distance, then seized a corner of her blanket, dragged it across the floor, dropped it on Laurie and wagged her tail hopefully. The child was so startled she stopped screaming.

"I think she's offering to play tug-of-war with you," Sharon said.

Laurie screwed up her face to resume screaming. Shaneen nosed the blanket closer. Laurie grasped a corner of it. Shaneen pounced on the opposite corner. Laurie pulled. Shaneen planted her back feet and tugged. The dog was stronger, but her paws couldn't get a purchase on the waxed floor. Shouting with laughter, Laurie dragged Shaneen around the kitchen until both fell in a tumbling heap.

That evening when Don Dykhouse came home and Laurie's hysterics began, Shaneen's barking almost drowned her out. "Hey, I saved your life," Don told the dog, but Shaneen had been trained to guard the young couple's baby, and Sharon had to take her by the collar, hold her and talk to her before Don could come into the house. After several nights of this, Laurie's hysterics stopped, as though observing the dog's fuss over nothing made her own seem silly, too.

One evening Don Dykhouse, pondering Timothy's inability to play, brought home the simplest toy he could find, a water pistol. Shaneen was lingering near as Don showed Tim how to fill it and squeeze the trigger. As the water arced through the air, the dog made a tremendous leap and tried to catch it. Tim crowed with amusement. He grabbed the pistol and fired it. Shaneen leaped again, and again. Don left the two of them playing happily together.

As well as loving water, Shaneen liked to fetch, and Steve obliged by throwing sticks for her to find and bring back. When Steve wasn't there, Shaneen dropped a stick at Tim's feet and wagged her tail hopefully, but Tim's attempts to throw the stick failed as it fell to the ground a few feet away, so one day he asked Steve to teach him how. They started with a tennis ball. Shaneen retrieved it when Tim threw it in a wayward direction, but as he got better, she began to jump for the ball and the game evolved into keep-away, with Tim and Steve throwing to each other and Shaneen in the middle trying to intercept the ball. Now, when supper was over, instead of disappearing, Steve began saying to Tim, "Come on, let's go outside and play with Shaneen."

At thirteen, Sherry was too dignified to romp and wrestle with the dog as the boys did. Intensely jealous of her privacy, she was suffering, as Sharon remarked to Don, from adolescent megrims. Shaneen seemed to sense this, and if she could nose Sherry's door open, she entered softly and laid her chin on the bed, not intruding but gazing at Sherry quietly until Sherry roused herself and called the dog to her for a hug.

The umpteenth time Sherry found black crayoned scraps among her most treasured possessions she screamed at Claire, "Don't you dare ever come in my room again! You're gross!"

For the first time Claire's smile faltered. She looked bewildered and hid in a corner. When Sharon went to see if she could persuade the girl to talk to her, she found her sobbing into Shaneen's ruff. "At least you like me," she whispered to the dog. Never before had the child let herself cry. From then on, whenever she was upset, it was Shaneen she turned to for comforting.

"It's as if we'd found the most wonderful nursemaid who knows when each child is troubled and just what that child needs," Sharon marveled to Don. "She senses when to be playful and when to be quiet, when to roughhouse and when to romp." She wanted to add that Shaneen was clear, as clear as a Wisconsin lake, and through her the poor, damaged children were learning that it was safe to trust, but she was afraid Don would think that fanciful.

"If she's so smart," Don grumbled, "why does she still treat me like the enemy? I saved her life and she won't even let me pet her."

One afternoon when Sharon was baking, Laurie and Claire and Tim hung over the counter waiting to lick the icing bowl. Laurie suddenly asked, "Is Shaneen foster or adopted?"

"Oh, adopted," Sharon told her. "Adopted means we're not just looking after her. She's ours. She's family."

"Even if she's bad, you won't send her away?"

"Never."

"You won't hurt her?"

"Never."

Claire said, "We're adopted."

"Yes," Sharon said. "Yes, you're adopted."

The children were silent until Laurie said, "I'll tell you what. After we've iced the cakes and the big kids come home, let's have a tea party with the pretty cups."

"Not me," said Tim. "Shaneen and me and Steve are going bear hunting in the woods."

Later, when Sharon was getting the blue luster teacups from the cupboard, she glanced out the window. The boys and the dog were running across the meadow and Tim was doing giant leaps. It crossed Sharon's mind that she had never seen a more carefree-looking boy.

On an evening soon after that, Sharon and Don took the six kids to the roller rink. All of them entered a limbo contest, but one by one they fell as they tried to slither under the ever-lower bar—all except Claire. "Hey, look at clunky Claire go," Sherry said as it became apparent the little girl had a chance to win. Quickly Sherry organized their bleacher row into a cheering section. "Go, Claire, go!" they chanted. Claire flushed, then grinned and waved. Cheered on by the encouraging shouts, she kept going until she was the last one left standing.

Sharon thought it was winning the trophy that made Claire's closed face suddenly look open and radiant, but when they got back to the house, she heard Claire shouting for Shaneen as she raced to be the first through the door. The dog instantly caught the child's excitement and leaped and barked as Claire delightedly told her, "They cheered for me, Shaneen! I've got friends! I've got friends!"

Often in the evenings the children would lounge on the floor in front of the fire, and always in their midst was Shaneen. Her favorite treat was popcorn, and she turned from one child to another to have a piece thrown in the air for her to catch and gobble down.

It was as though the kids were the spokes of a wheel, Sharon thought, watching them, and Shaneen, at the hub, linked them together. Through loving her, they were learning to love each other.

"Hey, kids, that's enough popcorn for the dog," Don cautioned them. He spoke her name. "Shaneen…"

She still came to him with some reluctance. But as the kids quieted and lay looking at the fire with their heads pillowed on each other, and as Don's fingers gently explored the tender spot behind her ears where she liked to be scratched, Shaneen settled herself closer and tucked her head into the crook between his neck and shoulder. Moments later Laurie nuzzled her way in between Sharon and Don and rested her head on Don's other shoulder.

Sharon and Don smiled at each other over the child's head. "She's made us a family," Don said softly.

"Thank you, Shaneen," Sharon said.

A Deer Asks for Help

The dog saw the deer first. Dropping into a crouch, he gathered himself to spring and run. This alerted Alison Millard, and she tightened her grip on the leash, pulling it taut to signal Topper that he was not to chase the deer.

She looked up, expecting to spot the white tail of the deer as it bounded off through the woods. To her surprise, the doe was standing perfectly still at the edge of the path about twenty yards ahead. It was half concealed in underbrush, but its forequarters were in the open and its head was turned toward Alison and the dog. It was staring fixedly in their direction.

It's hurt, Alison thought. *It's dazed.* She had seen that same stare on a deer grazed by a car on a nearby mountain road. For minute after minute the deer had stood unmoving in the middle of the road until an impatient motorist honked. Then, with a sudden shake of its head, the deer had come to its senses and leaped away into a field.

Alison clapped her hands sharply, expecting the same thing to happen now. Instead, the deer turned to look toward the path ahead, then back at Alison. The deer's eyes, Alison realized, were not blank, unseeing. They were focused, and there was something in them of a question. Or was it an appeal? Again, the deer turned its head just enough to indicate the path ahead before its steady gaze went back to Alison.

Alison had the clear impression the deer was asking her to follow it. *How strange,* she thought. *That sort of thing only happens in fairy tales.* The doe signaled again with a turn of its head to look along the path, then took a long look back at Alison. Alison hesitated. Should she follow? *What can happen?* she asked herself. *This isn't a bear or coyote. The deer isn't going to hurt me.* She tied Topper's leash to a tree and said, "Stay," quietly but firmly.

She started down the path toward the deer. When she was a dozen steps away, the deer moved off the path into the woods. Staying a bit ahead, it moved through the woods parallel to the path, turning its head every few steps to check that Alison was following. Alison, because she and Topper often walked this way, knew the path and knew that it passed a cottage tucked into the woods at the end of a long lane.

They were coming to it now. Alison could see the white picket fence in front of it. The doe stopped at the edge of the woods where the trees thinned out and waited until Alison drew even. When their eyes met, the doe shifted her gaze to the picket fence. Back to Alison. Back to the fence.

The fence was not high, only three feet or so. A deer could easily vault over it. Why was the doe staring at it and seeming to will

Alison to look at it, too?

Alison stepped free of the woods. She moved closer to the fence and ran her eye along it. Now she understood. Trapped between two of the pickets was a tiny fawn a few days old.

It was easy to guess what had happened. The mother had jumped the fence, and the fawn, too small to make the leap, had tried to run between two pickets and become wedged midway through. The doe had probably nosed the fawn and rumbled encouragingly in its throat as the fawn struggled, but the struggling had only wedged the baby more firmly, and there was nothing the mother could do to free it. So it had done the next best, but surprising, thing: when it heard Alison and Topper coming through the woods, the deer risked its own safety and asked for help.

The fawn panicked as Alison came near, kicking and thrashing. Alison knelt and caught its hindquarters to hold the tiny creature still. Her voice and touch were soothing, and when the fawn had quieted, she set to work tugging with all her strength at first one, then the other of the imprisoning pickets. There was no give to either; the wood was new and strong, the fence stoutly made. She found a sturdy stick and tried to wedge the pickets open an inch. They didn't move. Could she work a nail loose? She threw all her weight into the effort. Nothing budged.

If only she had a tool—a saw or crowbar or hammer. The couple who lived in the cottage were away all day at work. The house would be locked and Alison couldn't imagine breaking in to get a tool even on an errand of mercy. To walk to her own house to fetch a crowbar would take too long; the deer might well have abandoned the baby by the time she got back. She wondered if a passing car might have some sort of tool that could serve to pry a picket loose. She decided to walk out to the road.

She looked toward the woods, trying to pick out the silhouette of the deer against the pattern of trees. "I'll be back," she called toward the woods. "I'm going for help. I'll be back." Did the doe hear her? Was she still there? Would she understand? Alison kept looking over her shoulder as she started up the lane, searching for the slightest movement, but the woods were still and silent.

On the road it was long minutes before she heard a car coming, and then it was not a neighbor or a workman in a pickup, as she hoped, but a stranger, a man in aviator sunglasses driving a sleek black convertible. The man resettled the tweed cap on his silver-streaked hair as Alison hurried through an explanation of why she had stopped him. "A fawn?" he said, his voice rising. "You stopped me for a fawn?"

"I thought if you had a jack…"

"Changing a tire is not something I do."

"The handle of a jack. To use as a lever." Alison indicated the lane. "It's just down there.…"

The man scowled. "I've got an appointment. But okay, I'll take a look. Get in."

Get in a car with a man she'd never seen before and drive into the woods? Alison hesitated. The man's gloved hand drummed on the steering wheel. Alison thought about the risk the deer had taken to get help for her fawn. She got in the car.

At the house, the man left the motor running and strode toward the fence. "The jack?" Alison called after him. He didn't reply. Alison saw with alarm that the fawn's head was now hanging limply. She hurried through a gate in the fence and sank down to brace its head in her lap.

"Piece of cake," the man announced, surveying the situation. As Alison had done, he grabbed a picket and pulled. He jerked it, rattled it, yanked it. He pushed the picket on the near side of the fawn and pulled the one on the far side. He rocked the fence. He picked up the stick Alison had used, threaded it between the two pickets and yanked. The stick broke. Irritably he stepped back and set himself to kick, then looked down at his Italian-made shoes and thought better of it. He looked around. "What can I use?"

"If you have a tire iron in the car…" Alison started, but the man was already heading for a cairn of rocks at the side of the lane. He returned with the biggest one he could hold in one hand. "Stay out of the way," he ordered Alison. She assumed he was going to try to pound a picket loose. Instead, he took aim and crashed the rock into the center of one of the pickets holding the fawn fast. The picket fractured. Two more swift, hard blows broke it in half. Alison grabbed the bottom half and wrenched it aside. Her hands went under the fawn. She cradled it, speaking softly as she lifted it into her arms.

The man tossed the rock toward the woods. "That does it, right?"

"Yes. Thank you. Thank you very much."

"Made a mess of the fence."

"I'll get a carpenter to fix it," Alison said. "I know you're in a hurry…."

"Right." The man started for his car, then turned back and gestured at the fawn. "Is it going to be all right? What are you going to do with it?"

"I'm hoping its mother is still in the woods there."

The man reached into his pocket and held out a business card. "Let me know how it turns out," he said over his shoulder. "It's kind of a pretty little thing."

"I will. Thank you again."

Alison waited until the car was out of sight. Carrying the fawn, she went through the gate and knelt on the grass at the edge of the woods. When the drumbeat of the fawn's heart had slowed, she set the small creature on the grass, testing if its legs would hold it. The fawn, swaying, lifted its head and let out a small, seeking bleat. After a while, it bleated again, a little louder, a little panicky. There came from the woods a snort, a quick release of air through flaring nostrils, not close, but the fawn heard it and took a trembling step. Another. Another. Then it was bounding into the woods.

Alison collected the broken pieces of picket, wrote a note for the owners of the house, and headed for the path to liberate Topper and resume their walk. When she got home, she would call the number on the business card and leave a message that the story had a happy ending. The fawn was back with its mother.

Where's Bubba?

In Texas brush country near the Mexican border, Buddy Thorne, an ex-rodeo rider, was on his way to hunt rattlesnakes with a friend of his when the men spotted two small creatures. They were about the size of rabbits and they stood swaying unsteadily in the middle of the dusty track. "What are they?" wondered Buddy as he jammed on the brakes to keep from running over them.

As the men leaped from the pickup, the babies came tottering toward them. So young that one still had the umbilical cord attached, they were crawling with fleas and gaunt with starvation. "They're javelinas! Buddy exclaimed, pronouncing it "havelina" in the Spanish way. He dropped to his knees beside one. "Hey there, Bubba. You're really in bad shape, aren't you? Where's yo' mama?"

As a surveyor for a power company, Buddy had occasionally come upon small numbers of the miniature wild pigs foraging for cactus roots. Mild-mannered creatures, javelinas were so loyal to the pack that if a hunter shot one, the others stayed by it even at risk to their own lives. That's what made it so unusual that these two babies were on their own.

"They don't have a chance," Buddy said. "If they haven't starved to death by nightfall, the coyotes will get 'em." The babies nuzzled his boots hungrily. Buddy hesitated. "Oh, heck," he said, sweeping them up in his arms, "we can't just leave 'em here to die."

At a general store, the men bought flea powder, canned milk and nursing bottles, then cleaned and fed the tiny animals. Although the babies gained strength from the feeding, they were far too young to survive on their own. Again Buddy pondered what to do. Perhaps it was his own war experience, when severely wounded in combat he had prayed for rescue, that made him reluctant to abandon these creatures. "What d'ya say you take that one," he suggested to his companion, "and I'll look after Bubba here?"

Buddy wasn't sure what his wife, Patsy, and two teenage daughters would say when he arrived home in Corpus Christi with a baby javelina. But he needn't have worried. The minute he turned back the flap of his jacket and Bubba's trusting brown eyes peered out, they fell in love with the small creature. "Milk," Patsy decreed. "Warm milk right now. Kids, where's that old doll carriage of yours?"

While Patsy heated the milk, the girls settled Bubba in a nest of blankets in the doll carriage with a teddy bear to keep him company. That night they got up every two hours to feed him. The next day, and for many weeks thereafter, they wheeled him around in the carriage and carried him in their arms, talking and playing with him.

Bubba thrived on the love and attention. Soon he was romping with the girls and lying on the floor watching television with them. After graduating to solid food, he fell into the habit of pattering into Buddy and Patsy's room at six in the morning and tugging at the sheet. He didn't jump on the bed—one scolding taught him not to do that—but if pulling the sheet off didn't wake Buddy, the javelina butted the mattress until Buddy laughed and rolled out of bed to get him his breakfast.

After eating, Bubba joined the girls while they brushed their teeth. One morning, to tease him, they put a dollop of toothpaste on his nose. Relishing the taste, from then on Bubba sat beside them every morning while they scrubbed his tusks with a toothbrush of his own and allowed him to swallow the foam.

When it took just twenty-four hours to paper-train Bubba, Buddy pronounced him to be smarter than any dog or horse he'd ever known. Indeed, the day the family came home to find the television set on and Bubba sitting in front of it watching the screen, he declared Bubba to be a prodigy among animals. But when it never happened again, the family reluctantly concluded that Bubba had hit the on button accidentally.

The Thorne daughters were raising a lamb as a 4-H project, and when Bubba was six months old, he joined Kirby in a small shed in the backyard where there was hay to snuggle into and a heat lamp for chilly nights. The javelina and the lamb rapidly became fast friends, tirelessly playing a game in which Kirby butted Bubba and Bubba lumbered around the yard in pursuit of Kirby. A neighbor's dog, envying the fun, learned to jump the four-foot fence and join in.

Every morning Buddy cooked an extra portion of his own breakfast of bacon and eggs and toast for Bubba; in the evening when she was making dinner, Patsy also made a plate for Bubba, whether it was steak and vegetables, spaghetti or pork chops. If the family stopped at a fast-food place, a take-out order of fried chicken went home with them for Bubba.

Chewing slowly and reflectively, Bubba munched his way through supper, then stood at the back door waiting for dessert. If, by any chance, someone forgot to bring it, Bubba would still be standing there patiently at midnight. He loved ice cream and would open his mouth wide for one of the girls to feed it to him spoonful by blissful spoonful. For beer, too, he happily waited for a swallow to be poured down his throat. But his absolute favorite was chocolate.

"You're a chocoholic," Buddy accused him. "Why are you sniffing my pockets? What d'ya think's in there? Ah, you found 'em, didya?" And Buddy would laugh and pull out the chocolate malt balls he always carried as a treat for Bubba.

A neighbor in her eighties, knowing the javelina's weakness, often leaned over the fence and shared chocolate chip cookies with him. One night Bubba repaid her kindness by scaring off an intruder trying to jimmy her back door. Repeatedly throwing himself against the fence, Bubba made such a racket that the burglar ran out from under his cap in his haste to get away.

Ordinarily, however, Bubba was the most peaceable of creatures. Neighborhood children stopped on their way home from school to pet him. If Patsy laid a hand on his back and instructed him to lie down, he complied immediately. "When we were playing and he grabbed my arm in his mouth," Buddy remembers, "all I had to do was say 'ouch' and he let go." And when the games were over, Bubba liked nothing better than to lie with his head in a lap, having his ears scratched and falling asleep in his contentment.

Thinking back, Buddy says, "I'm sure other families have loved an animal like we loved Bubba. But I'm darned if I know of any."

"He was like one of our kids," Patsy adds. "We didn't do anything that we didn't think of Bubba." Her voice breaks and tears fill her eyes as she remembers the events of six months before.

Bubba had been with them ten years when a family from Kansas moved into the neighborhood. One day the young mother peered across several backyards, spotted Bubba and imagined he was a wild boar, a beast capable of charging through fences and attacking her children. She raced inside and called the city's Animal Control Department, which in turn notified the Texas Parks and Wildlife Department.

The first the Thornes knew of the complaint was when two wildlife agents appeared at their door asking to see their license to keep a wild animal. "But Bubba isn't a wild animal," Buddy explained. "He's always lived here." He described the circumstances under which he had found Bubba and brought him home to save his life.

"Doesn't matter," said the agents, insisting that a javelina, any javelina, is a wild animal and must be returned to the wild.

"But Bubba would die in the wild," Buddy protested. "He can't eat cactus roots and fight off coyotes. He doesn't know how."

Nevertheless, the agents said, it was the law.

"At least give me twenty-four hours," Buddy begged. "I've got a friend with a ranch. I'll take him there."

He and the agents were arguing the point when Patsy arrived home. Learning that the men intended to take Bubba, she burst into tears. "I wish I had a shotgun," she sobbed into Buddy's shoulder.

The agents, choosing to interpret her remark as a threat, marched through the house into the backyard. Bubba ran to greet them. Backing off, the men shot him with a tranquilizer gun.

Bewildered, Bubba struggled to reach Buddy. As Buddy knelt to gather him in his arms, Bubba lost consciousness.

The agents wrote out a summons for keeping a wild animal, dragged Bubba to their truck and drove off.

"If only I'd followed them," says Buddy. But he wanted to calm Patsy and he assumed the agents would hold Bubba for twenty-four hours, as was customary, before taking any action. The next morning, however, when he went to the Wildlife Department to argue again to be allowed to take Bubba to his friend's ranch, he was told the agents had tranquilized Bubba a second time, transferred him to the trunk of a car and driven into the country, where they had left him by the side of the road.

"Where?" Buddy pleaded. "Tell me where."

The agents refused. Buddy, indignant at their handling of the situation and frightened for Bubba's life, went to the newspapers. Radio and television reporters picked up the story. Suddenly Bubba was a *cause célèbre*. "High-handed," "insensitive," "bureaucratic foul-up," trumpeted editorials. "Pignapping," claimed callers to radio talk shows. Buddy and Patsy were interviewed on the nightly news. T-shirts with WHERE'S BUBBA? appeared as if by magic, and stickers with BRING BUBBA BACK and BUBBA CALL HOME sprouted on car bumpers all over town.

A week later, when Buddy and Patsy appeared in court on the misdemeanor charge of keeping a wild animal, the courtroom was filled with reporters, TV cameras and spectators; members of the Humane Society picketed outside. The Thornes' lawyer introduced into evidence snapshots of Bubba eating ice cream, standing on his hind legs to kiss Patsy and wearing a party hat. "Now, I ask you," the lawyer said to the presiding justice, "is a javelina who attends a New Year's Eve party a wild animal?"

"He is," insisted the Wildlife Department. The court ruled that although javelinas are wild animals, Bubba himself obviously was not. But the wildlife authorities still refused to tell where they had released the animal, and the court did not have the power to force them to reveal the information. Patsy and Buddy immediately filed suit in a higher court.

One week had already passed, and it would be three more before their suit could be heard. Desperately afraid that Bubba couldn't make it on his own that long, the Thornes spent every free moment combing country roads for him. People everywhere were also on the lookout. Calls came daily saying that a javelina had been spotted eating at a trough with domestic pigs, a friendly javelina had approached a party of picnickers, a javelina had been spotted hiding in a culvert. Buddy and Patsy drove hundreds of miles, sometimes getting up in the middle of the night when a report of a sighting came. But as many times as they shouted his name and searched and called again, no Bubba came trotting out of the brush to lay his weary head in their laps.

Interviewed repeatedly by the media, Buddy leaned over backward to be fair. "The last thing I want," he said, "is for people to hear how wonderful Bubba was and then go shoot a javelina so they can take her baby. Or take in an owl or a raccoon or any other animal to keep as a pet. Wild animals really do belong in the wild."

"But what if someone finds an injured or abandoned animal like you did?" he was asked.

"They should take it to a wildlife rehabilitator who is trained to care for an animal in such a way that it can be released back into the wild," Buddy answered. If he had it to do over, Buddy said, that's what he would do with Bubba. "But I didn't know then that rehabilitators existed," he said, "and I did what I thought was right at the time. My quarrel with the Wildlife Department now is the heartless way they've gone about this. If the authorities really cared about the animal, they wouldn't have left Bubba by the side of the road to starve."

The higher court agreed and ordered the Wildlife Department to supply the Thornes with a map showing where Bubba had been released. A volunteer pilot was standing by to make an air search. Hundreds more volunteers were poised to make a sweep on the ground. Buddy had posted a $1,500 bond against possible damage to private property by the searchers. Everything was in readiness for the moment the map would be turned over.

Instead of providing a map, the Wildlife Department filed an appeal.

Buddy and Patsy kept asking themselves why. The Wildlife Department must realize they were dooming Bubba by seeking this further delay. Was he already dead, killed by the second tranquilizing injection? Was that why the Wildlife Department was stonewalling?

The Thornes were never to know the answer.

In April, four months later, the Wildlife Department lost the appeal and finally handed over the map. No searchers were on hand then to help look for Bubba. No one believed he was still alive. But Buddy and Patsy hoped against hope.

They drove to the spot marked on the map. It was empty country. There was nothing as far as the eye could see—no house or barn Bubba might have gone to for refuge. It was useless for the Thornes even to get out of the car. But they did. Buddy stood with his arm around Patsy as they looked off to the far horizon. Finally Patsy said, "Is it because we loved Bubba so much that I feel he's still alive out there somewhere?"

Buddy nodded. "Maybe that's what love means," he said after a while. "You stay alive in the hearts of the people who loved you long after you're gone."

It is unlikely that the Thornes will ever know the end of Bubba's story. But because of Bubba and the outcry over his treatment, the Texas Parks and Wildlife Department has changed their policy. Now owners are allowed to place a wild animal who has become a pet in a location of their choice or, alternatively, to turn it over to a wildlife rehabilitation center, to be released only when and if it can survive in the wild. So, in one sense, Bubba's story does have an ending after all—a happy ending for other animals who, for one reason or another, have come in out of the wild.

Woman (and Dog) to the Rescue

The lady always wears a beeper on her belt or carries it in her pocketbook. A backpack and duffel bag are packed and ready in the bottom of her closet. On a moment's notice Caroline Hebard dons orange coveralls, buckles an orange vest on Aly, her German shepherd, and sets out for wherever in the world the two of them are needed.

Such a call came on a November day. Within forty-eight hours this slightly built woman with an elegant cut to her blond hair had left her husband and children far behind in their home in Bernardsville, New Jersey, and was crawling through collapsed buildings with the stench of death all about her in earthquake-ravaged Soviet Armenia.

"I've never seen such devastation," Hebard says. "Towns eighty to ninety-nine percent destroyed. Schools, factories, apartment buildings—everything flattened, pancaked. Leninakan, where we were, was a city of death—coffins stacked on street corners, piled in fields. And cold. Bitter, bitter cold. That's why we had so few live finds."

"Live finds" is how Caroline Hebard and the other volunteer members of the USAID disaster response team speak of still-breathing people they and their search dogs locate trapped under tons of rubble. Hebard tells of one such find in Leninakan: "A father pleaded with us to return to a building we'd already searched. Grief does funny things to people's senses, but he was so insistent he'd heard sounds that finally we went with him."

Searching is such a team effort that Hebard cannot now remember if she was the handler who located a way into the debris, gave Aly the order "Go find" and crawled in right behind him. In any event, one of the search dogs, with his handler on his heels, picked and squirmed his way through the rubble, tracking scents that drifted like smoke through cracks and crevices in the collapsed building. When the dog alerted, signaling a live find, a second dog and handler went in because the search component of the team never calls in the rescue component unless two dogs indicate a find; time is too precious to waste digging in an area only to come up empty-handed.

The second dog confirmed a live find. The rescue team went to work with cutting and lifting tools, and hours later an eleven-year-old girl, buried for four days alongside the dead bodies of her grandmother and brothers and sisters, was dug out from under masses of smashed concrete, miraculously unhurt except for broken ribs.

Hebard didn't witness the reunion of father and daughter, however, because as soon as the area of the find had been marked with orange tape, the search team moved on, racing to locate as many people as possible while there was still hope of getting them out alive. The searchers went for long stretches without sleep or food. Even the dogs shared in the sense of urgency, and Hebard had to coax Aly to eat and rest for fear he would drop with exhaustion.

The stamina of both dogs and handlers is severely tested in such chaotic emergencies as the Armenian earthquake, and Hebard sees to it that Aly stays in top-notch condition. His thick tan and black coat gleams with health; his brown eyes snap with interest and intelligence. Even for a German shepherd, Aly is a large dog, perhaps because he was imported from Germany, where breeding standards are rigorous. But despite his serious size and deep-chested bark, Aly, when not on duty, is a warm and friendly creature who greets a visitor with such a variety of gleeful rumblings he seems about to burst into speech.

Traveling on a search mission with Hebard, Aly attracts toddlers in airports who pull his tail and try to climb on his broad back, which he not only tolerates but appears to enjoy. By prior arrangement with the airlines, he travels in the passenger section with Hebard because, like all highly trained search dogs, he is much too valuable to be put at risk of a drop in temperature or pressure in the baggage compartment. Also, were he to be left in a crate on the tarmac to await loading, the fumes from the jet engines would render his keen sense of smell inoperative for at least twenty-four hours, which is time that cannot be lost in search and rescue work.

When they go into action, Hebard at a reed-slim five feet six inches and 105 pounds would seem no match for Aly in endurance. Yet she manages well on little sleep and keeps going day and night in circumstances that would floor a sinewy man. The daughter of a British diplomat, Hebard grew up in Chile, Venezuela, Argentina, Switzerland, Portugal, Turkey and Bahrain and speaks the languages of these countries, which is immensely helpful in international rescue operations.

In this and other ways, her life seems to have been almost uniquely molded to fit her for search and rescue work. As a teenager, when her father was posted to the British embassy in Washington, Caroline's hobby was exploring caves in the Virginia mountains. Then later, as a graduate student at Stanford University in California, she added rock climbing and wilderness backpacking to her interests. Because of her skill at rope techniques and at finding her way with map and compass, Caroline became someone called upon to join search parties when hikers disappeared in the High Sierra or climbers met with an accident.

She married a physicist who shared her love of wilderness, and they have four children. While they were living in California, she acquired two German shepherds. One, bred in Germany, had been trained in tracking, obedience and protection work, and Caroline thought it might be useful to understand Zibo's capabilities. Joining a group of law-enforcement officers being trained by an exacting instructor, also from Germany, she quickly displayed a special aptitude at handling dogs. When her husband's work brought the family east, one of the first things Caroline did was join a local unit of the American Rescue Dog Association.

Members of the association respond to situations in this country as varied as a missing child, a drowned white-water rafter or a police request to track a suspected murder victim. One of Caroline and Zibo's first searches took place in a small town in Virginia where the police asked for help in finding a senile old man who had wandered off and been missing for several days.

They were deep in the woods and Zibo was sniffing the air with interest when a radio message called off the search because of a severe thunderstorm alert. The next morning, although assigned elsewhere, Caroline said she had a feeling about where they'd been. She and Zibo retraced their steps, and Zibo, picking up a scent, ranged ahead of her. In minutes, he came racing back through the woods and snatched up a stick in his mouth, tail wagging madly.

Caroline followed him to a clearing but saw nothing. "Here?" she asked Zibo. "Where?" He put the stick down and nosed at the trunk of a tree. Stepping around it, Caroline saw that it was hollow, and inside, on a bed of leaves, lay the old man, suffering from exposure but alive.

Caroline radioed back for transport, and while they waited for it to arrive, she praised Zibo and threw the stick for him to fetch as his reward for a job well done. All the dogs are trained not to bark when they find someone lost in the woods for fear their sudden appearance will be totally unnerving to an already badly frightened person. Thus Zibo's signal to Caroline of mission accomplished is to bring her a stick, indicating he is about to earn his reward of having her play with him.

Training a dog to search starts when he is very young. "A puppy," says Caroline, "begins bonding to his owner immediately, so his instinct if his owner hides is to go looking for him. By increasing the distances, the dog learns to track, and by not letting him see the direction his owner has gone in, he learns to search." Caroline's preference is for German shepherds, but any working breed—that is, hunting or herding dogs—can be trained for search and rescue work. On the international team there are a Labrador, a giant schnauzer, a golden retriever, a rottweiler, a Doberman, an Australian cattle dog and two Newfoundlands.

"Each dog is different," Caroline notes, "and you have to observe him closely to learn whether you're being too tough and discouraging him or giving him too much praise and making him lazy." Hebard doesn't believe in harsh training and feels that women make particularly good handlers, "perhaps because our experience of raising children gives us patience and consistency." She observes, "Praise, reward and affection are what motivate a dog. For every ounce of correction, you should give nine ounces of love." As she says this, her hand reaches out to stroke Aly, and he takes a step closer to lean against her.

For a basic wilderness search, a year's training is required for both handlers and dogs. Twice a month they go through a daylong training session in a simulated disaster situation, and every three months there is a full weekend of training and evaluation. After basic training, the dog is taken to shopping centers to accustom him to noise and crowds. He learns to respond to hand signals as well as voice commands because he will often be working in high-noise situations, with bulldozers, cranes and power tools going full blast.

Each dog develops his own body language. When Aly scents a find, if the person is alive, he pricks his ears forward, wags his tail enthusiastically and digs at the rubble. If the person is close to death, he whines and moves his tail slowly, apparently basing his estimate on the scent of hormones such as adrenaline that the body gives off. If it is a dead find, Aly lets his tail droop dispiritedly.

Aly, who is six years old, will work until he is ten, by which time Hebard will have another dog trained and ready. Although Aly has a kennel and run outside that he shares with two other German shepherds, one retired from search work, he sleeps in the house in inclement weather. When the Hebard children come home from school, they play with him, and when dog and children are tired from wrestling and running, they stretch out on the floor of the family room, the children using Aly as a pillow while they watch TV.

The closest bond, though, is between Caroline Hebard and Aly, for they have gone through many dangers together—the threat of aftershocks in earthquakes, shifting debris in a pancaked building and mud slides following a flood. No dog is ever sent into an emergency situation alone. Hebard, wearing orange coveralls for visibility, a hard hat with a miner's lamp, boots, work gloves and often a mask to filter out dust, goes into the chaos close behind Aly, sometimes wriggling through jackstraw heaps of bricks and beams, sometimes deposited by the bucket of a crane on top of a mountain of crashed concrete.

"Concrete makes dust when it crumbles," Hebard observes, "and in the Bridgeport, Connecticut, office building collapse, it was raining. The dust turned to a slippery mud, and there we were, trying to climb around this massive mess of slabs tilted every which way. It was a hairy situation." As well as agility and stamina, searching for victims takes courage, which Hebard does not mention. What she does say is, "You can't be claustrophobic, and you've got to have a strong stomach. Sometimes a severed arm or leg is sticking out of the rubble. Sometimes you have to crawl right over a dead body."

In a flood disaster in Johnstown, Pennsylvania, Hebard, who was pregnant at the time, was assigned to search a trailer park buried in mud. "The reek of death was unimaginable," she comments, adding wryly, "It gave me a whole new definition of morning sickness." Later in that pregnancy and for several months afterward, she did not go on missions. Nor will she go now if one of her children is ill, a graduation is coming up or an important family occasion is planned. Family concerns come first, but her husband and children are extremely proud and supportive of her work, and she is fortunate to have a live-in housekeeper to keep the house running smoothly when she is away.

Why does Hebard do search and rescue work? "It takes a lot of dedication," she admits. "It's heartrending work. But also it's an adrenaline high full of drama, excitement and intense involvement. You're a highly trained professional, doing a job few people can do. There's great camaraderie among the team members—in freezing cold Russia, we put an American flag and a sign in front of our tents saying, 'Welcome to the Leninakan Hilton.'"

Hebard, who has a drawerful of awards, including a commendation from the Mexican government, has had advanced Red Cross training in first aid and CPR and is herself certified to train emergency medical technicians. Her most recent course was in critical incident stress debriefing. "We watch our team members closely for signs that they are being stressed by being exposed to so much death. When people stop communicating, become short-tempered, stop eating or sleeping, we deal with it right away by talking it out before it becomes a full-blown problem."

The work is entirely voluntary; there is no pay involved, and each person supplies his or her own equipment, which can run to considerable expense. Team members must have a special radio costing several hundred dollars, a beeper, a sleeping bag, a portable stove, boots, and so on. Lately the Alpo Corporation has been helping by paying for some of the equipment, underwriting airfares within the United States and sponsoring a national training seminar.

The best, most highly trained of the handlers and dogs are recommended by their local search and rescue units for the USAID disaster response team, which is co-directed by Hebard and Bill Dotson of Virginia and is under the auspices of the Office of Foreign Disaster Assistance (OFDA) of the State Department. Six of the eight handlers available to go to Armenia happened to be women, the majority of them women with jobs. Members of the team make advance arrangements with their employers to leave at a moment's notice when their services are needed.

Engineers and firefighters specially trained at extricating people from collapsed buildings are also part of the team, as are physicians skilled in treating trauma. Altogether the team numbers about thirty people and is self-sufficient in everything except ground transportation and fuel. Food for the team is military rations supplied by the U.S. government; food for the dogs is a high-energy puppy ration supplied by Alpo.

Transport is arranged by the OFDA and is by the fastest means available, whether military, commercial or chartered plane. "In the El Salvador earthquake," Hebard remembers, "we got in quick and saved thirty-seven people in a matter of hours.

"The thing of it is," she goes on with a touch of regret in her voice, "the local people have rescued the victims who can be seen or heard by the time we get there. We find people who haven't been detected, and alas, that means a great deal of our work is body finds, not live finds."

The generally poor odds make an experience such as rescuing twelve children lost on the Appalachian Trail that much more rewarding. It was late at night and the temperature had dived to ten degrees when Aly and Hebard set out with Park Service rangers to hunt for the little band. There was no question of waiting for daybreak, for people can die of exposure quite quickly. "Anyway," says Hebard, "I'd rather search at night. Scent travels farther and people tend to stay put, so it is easier to find them."

Out on the trail, Caroline spotted footprints in a muddy patch that had frozen. That told her the direction the children had gone, and she instructed Aly to use a tracking mode, nose to the ground, rather than a scenting mode, nose in the air. Miles later the trail crossed a road, and a ranger said, "Okay, now all we have to figure out is whether they turned north or south on the road."

"Neither," said Caroline, watching Aly. "They continued on the trail." Sure enough, two miles farther on, Aly began wagging his tail enthusiastically. Rounding a bend in the trail, they came upon the huddled children, desperately cold and badly frightened but otherwise all right. Even at two in the morning, Aly got his reward of playing with a stick, as well as a hug from Hebard and quickly whispered words of praise.

Caroline's face lights up as she tells this story. It is infinitely more satisfying to find twelve children alive than, for example, frozen bodies in Leninakan or the drowned bodies of people swept downstream in the Schoharie Creek Bridge disaster on the New York Thruway. But whatever the catastrophe, the lady and her dog are mission-ready at all times to go anywhere in the world to give the help they are uniquely qualified to provide.

How Do You Spank a Duck?

They were the two dirtiest ducks Kay Sherwood had ever seen. Large and white with warty red faces, they were sipping water from a mud puddle in the hay field across the road from her house, and every time they raised their heads to let the water slide down their throats, the mud flowed down their necks like lava. Kay had gone out in her front garden to cut June roses for the dinner table, and when the ducks caught sight of her, they decided to see if she would feed them and came waddling across the road. She shooed them away. Keen about gardening, the last thing Kay wanted was to have two flat-footed ducks trampling her flower beds.

The next morning as she was getting breakfast she glanced out the window. The ducks were in her raspberry patch, snapping up the reddest, ripest berries. Grabbing a saucepan and a slotted spoon to bang it with, Kay hurried out the back door making a terrific clatter. The ducks rushed a dozen steps off, decided she was bluffing and plodded resolutely back to the raspberry patch. Kay whistled for her dog. Barking furiously, the dog retreated steadily across the lawn as the ducks advanced on him, hissing and bobbing their heads menacingly. Obviously Kay would have to use strategy, not force, to rid herself of the ducks. She fetched a box of saltines from the house. Scattering broken crackers as she went, she enticed the ducks around the house, across the road and back to the hay field.

That taught the pair of them a lesson. Unfortunately, the lesson was not to stay out of the raspberry patch but to make a feint toward it so Kay would rush out of the kitchen door with crackers for them. Kay had to concede they had won that round, but she was determined not to be lured into making friends with them. Nor would she by any means allow them to settle down in the daylily bed just because they had decided it was a shady spot from which to keep sharp eyes fixed on the back stoop for her appearance.

The only problem was…how do you spank a duck?

The ducks took up residence in the daylily bed, and whenever Kay came out of the house, they rose majestically and came waddling toward her as fast as they could slap one webbed foot down in front of the other. Watching them approach one day, almost tumbling in their haste but with something about them as stately as dowagers, Kay laughed at how much they looked like two venerable great-aunts of hers. The ducks had won another round; they now had names—Phyllis and Annie.

But which was to be Annie, which Phyllis? There was not a wart's worth of difference in their scarlet beaks, their tiny brilliant eyes, their overall size and shape. All Kay was really sure of was that one was always perceptibly muddier than the other, so she became Dirty Annie. And Phyllis shortly became Philip when, abandoning the pretense that she wasn't growing ridiculously fond of her presumptuous guests, Kay reached out to stroke Dirty Annie's feathered neck. Philip stopped eating, fixed her with a sharp look, and hissed. "Ah, she's yours, is she?" Kay said, suddenly realizing that, of course, they were a pair.

Once aware of that, Kay began noticing how their behavior differed. Philip always took the lead in their excursions across the road, through the fields and down to the river, while Dirty Annie was quicker to go to people. It was she who stood on Kay's feet to reach a cracker in her hand. It was she who followed close behind when Kay picked raspberries and gave her jeans a sharp tweak when Kay was slow to share the berries with them. It was she who ate the quarter pound of Brie cheese Kay put out on the terrace table when guests were coming for a drink; Kay knew it was Annie because Annie was wearing the wrapper around her neck like a ruff. And it was Annie who flapped up on that same low terrace table, skidded across its tiled top and plumped herself down in Kay's lap for her afternoon nap—which made Kay forgive her all her other transgressions.

The better Kay got to know the ducks, the more paradoxical she found them. They had wings but never flew. They had webbed feet but never swam (Philip went in the river to bathe once a day, but Dirty Annie seldom went near the water). They were inseparable but seemed quite willing to seriously wound each other over a cracker. They were ducks but they did not quack. They were defenseless but afraid of nothing. They were fiercely independent but followed Kay everywhere.

During the day their greatest pleasure was to have her weed the garden. As she worked along a row, they kept a sharp eye out, and when she uncovered a bug or beetle, they snapped it up. When she uncovered a worm, all three of them pounced, Kay to save it for the good of the garden, the ducks to pull it wriggling from the earth. Seldom did Kay win; often did she get her knuckles sharply rapped for interfering.

Although their days were spent at Kay's house, Annie and Philip slept at night in a hollow on the riverbank. In the morning they crossed the road, circled the house and patrolled at the foot of the kitchen steps until breakfast was forthcoming. In the late afternoon they crossed to go to the river for Philip's bath, then returned to the house at dinnertime. For reasons Kay never fathomed, they considered that supper, unlike breakfast, came via the front door, and they waited at the bottom of the porch steps for it to appear. If it was delayed, Dirty Annie tried to climb the steps, slapping a webbed foot on the edge and falling on her face as her foot slipped off. Finally, with a great flailing of wings, she would manage to scramble up, whereupon she would march to the screen door, rap sternly upon it with her beak and peer beady-eyed into the dark interior until Kay appeared with slices of bread and a handful of lettuce leaves.

Their routine was so unvarying that Kay began to worry when one twilight came with no sign of them. She walked down the road calling their names. Finally she spotted a patch of white and hurried toward it, dreading to find that one or both had been hit by a car.

Dirty Annie was standing on the riverbank by herself. When she saw Kay, she began to bob her head—her distress signal. Kay ran to her. Then she saw Philip. He was in the river, close to the far bank. As Kay hesitated, he gave a mighty thrash of his wings and sank down exhausted. He was drowning.

Kay plunged into the river, clothes, shoes, wristwatch and all, and half waded, half swam across. Reaching Philip, she snatched him up in her arms. And she saw what had happened. He wasn't just entangled in submerged branches, as she had supposed. One webbed foot was held fast in the jagged jaws of a muskrat trap.

As soon as she freed him, Philip paddled straight across to Dirty Annie. Face-to-face on the bank, they bobbed their heads at each other over and over, quite as though Philip was expressing his relief at being rescued and Dirty Annie was scolding, *I told you not to go near the water.*

Not long after that, it was Philip's turn to come to the rescue of Dirty Annie. Late one night Kay went out on the porch to call the dog. What answered her call was a puppy, a Siberian husky, obviously lost and ecstatic at finding someone to take him in. In the morning when Kay went out to feed the ducks, the puppy tumbled through the door behind her and was after the ducks before she could stop him. Philip scattered one way, Dirty Annie another.

The puppy, barking madly, cornered Dirty Annie. Philip halted, registered Dirty Annie's plight and waddled hastily back. For an instant he wavered, eyeing the wriggling, noisy puppy, then made up his mind. With a huge flap of his wings, he leaped on the puppy's back and pecked at his head. The puppy, yelping, ran. Philip balanced on his back as long as he could, and when he fell off, he spread his wings and gave chase on tiptoe.

Kay thought Philip's near drowning might have made him afraid of the river, but as the summer grew oppressively hot and she took to floating on the river on an air mattress with the dog swimming beside her, Philip joined them, paddling in lazy circles around the drifting mattress. Every so often there would be a rustling on the bank and Dirty Annie's head came poking through the tall weeds to peer at their progress, but nothing would entice her into the water.

As August rounded into September, increasingly Kay fretted about Dirty Annie and Philip and the coming winter. Soon she would be coming to the country only on weekends. Had they become dependent on her feeding them? Could they survive on their own? She decided not to risk it. She would put them in the car and take them to the village. People fed a flock of wild ducks by the river there, and Dirty Annie and Philip could join the flock and be sure of enough to eat.

One fine morning she filled a pie plate with bits of bread and tucked two pillowcases under her arm. As soon as the ducks were busy eating, she tried to slip a pillowcase over Annie's head. Annie squawked in alarm. Philip rushed at Kay, beak at the ready. Kay abandoned that plan. She got planks, fashioned a ramp into the car and spread bread crumbs on it. The ducks rapped on the planks with their bills and snapped up the crumbs as they rolled down. Kay's last idea was to place a whole loaf of bread in the car, with the door invitingly open. Dirty Annie and Philip, their heads bobbing, consulted each other and went off to sleep in the daylilies.

Well, she was going to Maine. They'd be on their own for ten days, and she'd see how they fared for that length of time. It was nighttime when she arrived back. She walked down to the river and there they were, asleep in their usual spot, their feathers gleaming whitely in the dark.

The next morning the ducks appeared at the kitchen door for their breakfast at the usual time. Kay hurried out to feed them, and just as always, Dirty Annie stood on her feet in her eagerness to get more than her share. Just as always, they supervised a last weeding of the garden. And just as always, Annie flopped in Kay's lap for her afternoon nap. Looking down at the beautiful tracery of feathers on her neck, Kay wondered for the thousandth time that summer why she had never heard or read of what wonderful companions ducks make. Philip and Dirty Annie were as intelligent as any animal, with the advantage of having extraordinarily acute vision and hearing—nothing, inside the house or out, escaped their notice. And they were as friendly as the dog while being equally as good watchdogs since they stood up and flapped their wings at the first sign of anyone's approach.

Because they had fared so well through Kay's ten-day absence, she was not concerned about leaving them the next week when she returned to the city, and she did not check that their whiteness was there in the dark when she arrived back late Friday night. She let the dog out Saturday morning, thinking this would signal them to come for breakfast. But nine o'clock came and went and the ducks did not appear. At ten Kay went looking for them. They weren't in the field. They weren't on the riverbank.

Twice more that day she searched, and along about twilight she spotted them. They were far down the road. When she got within earshot she called their names. They did not turn their heads. When she drew close, they moved uneasily. She held out a cracker and they backed away. They were afraid of her.

All day Sunday and again the following weekend Kay watched and hoped, but they did not come to the house. She took food to them twice a day, but they would not eat from her hand nor let her get near. Not wanting to add to their obvious distress, she put the food on the ground and went away.

Each time she passed their former sleeping place on the riverbank, she reminded herself she must collect the litter left by fishermen. Finally she remembered to bring a garbage bag, and after collecting soda cans, sandwich wrappers and bait containers, she moved on a few steps to where white feathers were caught in the tangled grass. The ducks' nest was filled with broken glass. Green beer bottles, difficult to see among the grass, had been smashed and scattered there. She had to fetch gloves and a rake before she could be sure the area was clear.

That night Philip and Dirty Annie were back in their nest. As soon as they were over their fright, they would be friends again, Kay was sure. But the following weekend, to her horror, she arrived to find the front yard full of feathers. The feathers were not the down the ducks customarily shed but large wing and tail feathers. A fox? Raccoon? Car?

She was searching for their bodies when a car stopped. "Looking for the ducks?" a neighbor asked. "A lady who lives on the mountain road has them in her garage because some kids pulled out most of their feathers."

Several times Kay went up the mountain to see how Philip and Annie were faring, but there was never anyone home and two large German shepherds kept her from going near the garage. Then one day in the spring, when she reopened her house after the winter, she was driving along the mountain road and saw the woman who had sheltered the ducks raking her front lawn. Kay stopped and asked if she still had the ducks.

"They got out a few weeks ago," the woman said, "but the kids have seen them back in the woods." She led the way through a field and into a stand of trees where a little creek ran. And there was Dirty Annie. Kay called, and Annie came to her. "You want her back?" the woman asked. "I'll get my husband to bring her down."

Kay spent that day and the next searching for Philip but found no trace of him. When Dirty Annie arrived in a big cardboard box, Kay carried her to the back of her land, on the riverbank but away from the road, hoping she'd find a place to nest there out of sight of passersby.

Released from the box, Annie, shifting nervously from one foot to the other, eyed the river. Suddenly making up her mind, she launched herself awkwardly into the air and splashed down in the river, where she proceeded to take an energetic bath. Clearly, a winter without washing had been too much even for Dirty Annie. When she was snow-white again, she climbed out on the bank and for the next two hours, while Kay came and went in her search for Philip, she preened her feathers.

When all was in order, Annie stood gazing at the river. Kay offered her some crackers. She snapped them up absently. Then, as though she had arrived at a decision, she again catapulted herself into the water. The current caught her and swept her downstream. Over the rocks she went, under the bridge, until, paddling strongly now, she came to the spot where she and Philip had nested the previous summer. She climbed out on the bank and settled into the hollow.

There she stayed. Kay ached for her aloneness without Philip and sometimes wondered if Annie blamed her for it, because her old cheerfulness was gone. When Kay took food to her, she marched in ever-tightening circles around her and pecked at Kay's feet. And one day she charged her. When she was quite certain she had driven her off, she made her way into a thicket beside the hollow and, fluffing her feathers, settled down carefully. Kay crept close enough to peer through the bushes. Dirty Annie was sitting on a new nest.

Kay had given up hope that Philip was still alive. But now her heart lifted. Dirty Annie would raise their ducklings, and one day in June Kay would look up from her gardening and there would be Dirty Annie marching across the road. Her ducklings, single file behind her, would be hurrying to keep up. Kay had no doubt they would head straight for her raspberries. Next time she went to the store, she must remember to lay in a good supply of crackers.

Connie and the Dog

When Connie Carey was a child, what she wanted most in the world was a dog. But her parents wouldn't hear of it. "A dog in the city? Never!" her mother decreed. "Out of the question!" her father confirmed. They were loving parents, however, so Connie did not give up hope. She kept the subject alive, and the day her smiling father came home early and announced he had a wonderful surprise, Connie let out a whoop of joy.

"A puppy!" she yelled, racing out in the hall to look for it. "Where is it? Is it all mine? Can I name it?"

"Come back here," her father ordered. "You've been told over and over, no dog."

"But you said you had a wonderful surprise."

"I do. You have a baby brother."

"Oh."

The load of disappointment in that single syllable became a running joke in the family, and Connie still sends her brother birthday cards teasingly reminding him that she would have preferred a dog.

Why didn't Connie get a dog when she was grown and making her own decisions? Well, first there was college, then graduate school, then years of teaching abroad. But finally she was living in a country house and she asked her friend Pat to go with her to choose a dog at the local ASPCA.

She was drawn to an aged, spindly-legged apricot poodle who shook with nerves, but Connie accepted Pat's word as an experienced dog owner that a black puppy with three white socks and a white tip to his tail was a better bet. "Look at his head," Pat urged. "It's beautifully shaped, and he has the coloring of a border collie. He'll be smart." So the black and white puppy was adopted and christened Charlie, and Connie got a book from the library about the training of dogs.

After a while she acquired two more books, for she didn't seem to be making much headway with Charlie. He was an exuberant, sweet-natured pup who was happy to cooperate for the length of his very short attention span; after that, he danced around her just out of reach, barking a cheerful song of defiance. When Pat witnessed this noisy fandango, after she stopped laughing she offered to take over because she was the one who knew how to handle dogs.

Charlie somehow mistook Pat's patient instruction as offers to play, and she couldn't make him behave any better than Connie could. It appeared she had been wrong in predicting his intelligence and had quite failed to spot his streak of willfulness. In desperation, Connie hired a trainer to come to the house.

The trainer, a broad, flat lady with iron-gray hair, arrived with three Pomeranians marching in formation at her heels. At a word from her, all three dogs leaped straight in the air, executed a 180-degree turn, came down facing in the opposite direction and stood at attention. Obviously, Charlie was about to meet his match.

He thought so, too. *"Achtung!"* the trainer snapped. "Heel!" Charlie dutifully placed himself on her left and marched beside her, up and down, out and back, wheeling smartly at the turns. "Charlie knows," the lady announced. "Now you." She handed the leash to Connie. *"Nein!* Not right! Not right!" After twenty minutes of shouted scolding, Connie, bathed in sweat and humiliation, turned the leash over to Pat. Now it was Pat's turn to have scorn heaped on her head.

"Nothing wrong with Herr Charlie," the trainer announced as the dog once again obeyed her every order to sit, lie down, roll over and speak. She pocketed her $75 fee and marched her Pomeranians out the door, muttering darkly, "The owner. Always the owner."

As soon as she left, Charlie affably denied working knowledge of how to do a single one of the desirable things he had done for the trainer. While he danced and barked, Connie looked at Pat. "Be careful what you wish for," she quoted wryly. "You may get it. All my life I wanted a dog, and now there's nothing I want less."

But she and Charlie rubbed along together until the day she came home to find that the dog not only had mistaken one of her shoes for a rawhide bone but had ripped the leather cover off a prized family Bible. Connie marched to the phone, dialed the ASPCA, and stated her intention to return a dog that had come from there. "All right," the attendant said, "but you'll have to wait until we have room for him. We'll call you as soon as we can take him."

Although Connie still claims that Charlie understood her end of this conversation, it was undoubtedly just coincidence, plus the fact he was about to turn a year old, that he began mending his wild ways. Overnight he started paying attention when spoken to, soon was behaving so well on walks that he could be let off the leash to run in the fields, responded immediately to a whistle, chewed only his own food and was so impeccably housebroken that to be outdoors was not enough; he had to be outdoors at what he considered a sufficiently tactful distance from the house. Most touching of all, he fell in love with Connie. From being just another object in his world, she became his world. He did not voluntarily let her out of his sight, and now his funny dance was used not to defy her but to express his delight when she came home to him.

As their companionship deepened, Connie wondered what she would say when the call came from the ASPCA. Then one day it dawned on her that it was never going to come, that the ASPCA knew dogs and people and a thing or two about the love between them and how it grows.

"Isn't he beautiful?" Connie remarked to Pat as Charlie moved into being full grown, with a plumed tail, silky fur and that handsome head. "I mean, besides being a great companion, he's a delight to look at."

"Be careful what you wish for," Pat teased. "You may get it."

"Yes, I know I said that." Connie was silent for a moment, thinking. "The thing of it is, sometimes it takes quite a while before you realize you really have gotten what you wanted after all."

The Owl Release

Guests who excuse themselves at Frances and Ben Robertson's house are apt to be gone quite a while, waylaid by a fascinating sight. The way to the powder room is through a hall that has French doors to a terrace across one side. Beyond the terrace is an expanse of lawn rimmed by woods, and in the center of the lawn is a feeding station, a roofed but open-sided summerhouse sheltering bins of corn and grain.

During the day, ducks and Canada geese advance on the bins in a stately waddle, while at night raccoons, possums, skunks, deer and an occasional fox feed there, undeterred by the floodlighting that allows them to be seen from the house.

On a winter night, as Mindy Schiffman passed through the darkened hallway, she glimpsed a largish shape against the snow, and on her way back from the powder room, she picked up a pair of the binoculars the Robertsons kept on a table in the hall and focused them on the shape. It was, as she had assumed, a deer, a small doe not a great deal larger than a hound.

Another turn of the focusing dial brought the doe's head so sharply close that she seemed only two or three feet in front of Mindy. Mindy smiled at the longing she felt to reach out and stroke the doe's sleek neck and was lowering the glasses when her attention was arrested by a dark mass near the doe's shoulder.

It was globular, the size of a grapefruit, a part of her yet hanging on her like some sucking creature. It was a mass of dried, blackened blood and fur and skin, a macabre snowball that had struck but not fallen. It was her flesh ripped and churned by bullets.

She's got a chance, Mindy thought. *If nothing reopens the wound, she'll make it.* She moved the glasses down the doe's length, and cried out. The doe's hind leg on the opposite side had been shot away. There was nothing below the knee joint; the leg ended in midair in another coagulated mass.

As though she had heard Mindy's cry, the doe turned her head toward the house and Mindy met her eyes in the glasses. Mindy had nursed her beloved Persian cat when she was broken by a car, held her springer spaniel while he died, and been struck at seeing only acceptance in their eyes. It was she who had railed against their pain, as she was railing now.

Frances came into the hallway and, reading Mindy's face, picked up another pair of glasses. When she saw what Mindy had seen, she lowered them and turned away to fumble for a handkerchief. When she turned back, she said, "The poor thing can't dig in the snow for food with that damaged front leg. She'll only starve to death if we let her go on like this."

While Frances went to speak to Ben, Mindy stayed on in the shadowy hallway, reluctant to return to the candlelight and laughter of the dining room. She thought of a line from *Hamlet,* "I must be cruel only to be kind," and wished it were a world in which paradox did not reign, in which it was possible simply to be kind in order to be kind.

Sometimes it is, of course. In this same house, six months earlier, twenty guests had listened to a powerful, rough-clad man talk joyously of his work with injured raptors. Broken-winged and broken-legged hawks, eagles and owls hurt in encounters with wires, cars or guns are brought to Len Soucy from all over the Northeast, and he, in his compound on the edge of the Great Swamp near Morristown, New Jersey, sets about mending them. When they become strong again at the broken places, he makes a ceremony of releasing the birds, inviting people who support his work to share in his delight at restoring them to the wild.

On a night when a full moon had risen over the pond in front of the Robertsons' house, Len Soucy led the way outside to where a stack of crates waited. In the light of flaming torches, he reached into a crate and brought forth a red-shouldered hawk in his gauntleted hand. "Who wants to release him?" he asked.

A boy of eleven or twelve volunteered, putting Mindy to shame, for she was afraid of the wicked glance and the curved talons of the hawk. One by one, as Len Soucy brought out the raptors, a guest stepped forward, donned a gauntlet and, grasping a raptor by the legs, held it aloft and released it into the night sky. But Mindy hung back, happy to leave the experience to others.

Finally there was one bird left, a great horned owl, the largest of the raptors and the fiercest looking. Len Soucy cautiously reached into the crate and grasped the creature's legs. His eyes went around the circle. "Who hasn't released one? You haven't," he said, singling out Mindy. His assistant handed her a gauntlet. Reluctantly Mindy slipped it on and, following instructions, placed her hand over Len's, her forefinger between the owl's legs, and closed her hand gently but firmly around the legs. Len withdrew his hand and stepped back.

Mindy moved outside the circle of light, facing the pond. There was only the darkness of the night sky and the moonlight on the water and the great horned owl. The owl at the end of her outstretched arm was…as light as a feather! That beetle-browed, glaring creature well over a foot tall weighed only ounces in her hand. His bones were hollow, his bulk was air, his being as fragile as thistledown in the wind. The power was all hers.

She raised the great bird high. "Go," she exulted. "Go and be free!" She tossed him at the moon. He spread his wings and soared.

Frances came back. "Ben's called the deputy who patrols for us during the hunting season," she said. "He'll be here in a few minutes."

Ben joined them. He swore softly as he looked through the glasses. "A doe, that's illegal. Hunting on private property, that's illegal. That's why she got away. The hunter was afraid to go after her for fear we'd spot him."

They heard the deputy's car coming up the long drive. The deer heard it, too, and raised her head sharply. "Don't run, don't run," Ben pleaded quietly. "It's better this way." The deputy cut his lights and motor and coasted in. The doe went back to eating. But she was wary now and kept lifting her head to listen. Somewhere out there was a man preparing to kill her. Her eyes turned to the house, and again it seemed, in the intimate glasses, that she was looking into their eyes, asking the fathomless question, *Why?*

Why? they echoed silently.

Because there are two factions in the world: the protectors and the destroyers. This night the destroyers had forced Mindy and Frances and Ben over to their side. What might bring the destroyers over to their side? If not a doe's eyes, what?

The sound was like the crack of a whip. The deer leaped. The gallant creature tried to run on three legs. Five bounds toward the safety of the woods. Her wounded front leg crumpled. She somersaulted to the ground. She twitched and lay still.

Her right to live on this beautiful earth had been taken from her. All Mindy could hope now was that they had released her spirit. "Go," Mindy whispered. "Go and be free."

The Good Shepherd

Lana Crawford sat numbly at the kitchen table. Her life in Klamath Falls, Oregon, once so happy, lay in ruins. Her marriage was over and the yellow house she loved had a For Sale sign in the front yard.

Reaching to stroke the German shepherd at her feet brought fresh tears to Lana's eyes. This special animal had been Jeremy's dearest friend and companion in the final days of her teenage son's life. "Oh, Grizzly," she moaned softly, "what will you and I do now? How do we go on?"

Two years earlier Jeremy, a running back and karate practitioner, had been unable to get up after being tackled in a football game. X-rays of his pelvis revealed bone cancer, and the teenager, once muscular and tan, grew pale and hollow-cheeked as he fought for his life.

Lana gave up her job as a music teacher to care for him, and his older sister, Susanne, traveled often from her home in Seattle to spend as much time as possible with him. They tried hard to keep him cheerful and optimistic, and Jeremy struggled valiantly against his pain and exhaustion. Trying to think of something that would please him and knowing that he had always had a special fondness for German shepherds, on a day between chemo treatments Lana suggested to Jeremy that they visit a kennel specializing in the breed. As they sat on a bench in the sun outside the dog runs with Ella Brown, the kennel owner, a litter of puppies tumbled and played at their feet. One of the puppies came to Jeremy. Jeremy picked him up and held him in his arms. "He's so beautiful," Jeremy said. "But why is he whimpering, Ella? Doesn't he like me?"

"That's his way of talking," Ella Brown explained. "Every once in a while there'll be one special dog in a litter who's a talker. That special dog deserves to go to a special person who will understand and cherish him. I think that might be you, Jeremy. Why don't you take him home and see if I'm right that you two belong together?"

Jeremy named the puppy Grizzly, and Ella was right: boy and dog quickly became inseparable. Jeremy understood all the small sounds Grizzly made in his throat, and Grizzly became attuned to the shades of meaning in Jeremy's voice, face and gestures. On days Jeremy was feeling well enough, they took long drives in Jeremy's little pickup or he threw his football in long spiral passes and Grizzly raced to jump and intercept it. On the not-good days, Jeremy dozed in bed and Grizzly lay quietly beside him, his body pressed close.

Grizzly could sense when it was pain keeping Jeremy in bed and when it was discouragement. When it was discouragement, Grizzly nosed Jeremy's hand and woofed deep in his throat until Jeremy began to talk to him, confiding his fear that he would never get well. As Jeremy's condition worsened, Lana spent the nights on the floor beside his bed. Grizzly tucked himself in beside her, and the two of them dozed through the long hours. Once when Jeremy woke up, he said to his mother, "If I don't make it, I want you to have Grizzly. Maybe there'll be some way the two of you can help other kids."

In the days following Jeremy's death, Lana lay in bed, unable to face life without her son. One afternoon she heard Grizzly nose open her closet door. A moment later he laid one of her running shoes on her pillow. He fetched its mate and began woofing encouragingly. The dog took her sleeve in his mouth and gently tugged. "I can't, Grizzly," Lana told him. But each day Grizzly tried again, until a day came when Lana followed him and they walked around the block. Each day after that he led her farther, and Lana began to grow strong again.

In the fall they came upon a park where boys were playing football. One of them was as tall and blond as Jeremy, and Lana remembered the promise she had made to her son. At age thirty-eight, she decided to move to Utah and enroll in the university there to take courses in psychology. As part of the fieldwork for her degree, Lana proposed that she take Grizzly to visit patients on the pediatric floor at the University of Utah Health Sciences Center.

She was nervous as a nurse led them to the room of a boy with cystic fibrosis. The boy was crying as a technician drew blood and hooked him up to an IV. The nurse asked the boy if he would like to meet Grizzly. His eyes widened. "A dog! Come here, Grizzly." The needles were forgotten as the boy talked to Grizzly and Grizzly responded with his soft, muffled woofs. "He's answering me! Can I take him for a walk?" Down the hall they went, IV pole and all.

Soon Lana and Grizzly were going to the hospital for weekly visits, and Grizzly seemed to know exactly how to respond to each ill child, whether to romp or lie with his head in a lap, to allow his ears to be pulled or nuzzle the child's ear and make her giggle, to woofle or give tiny, teasing barks. Lana could not explain his intuition except to say that Grizzly, through having loved Jeremy, seemed to understand his purpose in life to be to respond to pain and fear and need.

One day they visited a seventeen-year-old boy in the oncology unit. The severely depressed boy, who was losing his vision and muscular control, looked devastatingly like Jeremy. "This is Grizzly, the good shepherd," Lana said, telling herself that if she could get through this, she could get through anything. Grizzly was as shaken as she was, she saw, but when the boy asked for Grizzly to come up on the bed beside him, the dog hesitated only briefly before climbing up on the draw sheet the nurse spread and inching between the tubes to lie beside the boy. There he stayed, never moving, until the boy fell asleep.

As Lana was asked to go to different children's facilities with Grizzly, she became aware that the need for animal-assisted therapy was greater than she and Grizzly could meet alone. She formed a nonprofit organization, the Good Shepherd Association, to train handlers and their animals to work in therapeutic settings, and the association soon became an affiliate of the worldwide Delta Society, a volunteer, nonprofit society providing animal-assisted therapy.

At a center for emotionally troubled children, Lana and Grizzly met Tammy, an unkempt eleven-year-old who had been in and out of fourteen foster homes and centers, displayed extreme mood swings and fought with other children. She refused to say a word to Lana and paid no attention to Grizzly until, midway through the hour, Grizzly stood up, walked out into the hallway and began his gentle woofing talk. "What's he doing?" Tammy demanded.

"Maybe he's asking you to come out in the hall," Lana suggested.

Tammy tossed her head contemptuously, snatched up a doll and twisted its legs until she tore them off. But as Grizzly continued to talk, curiosity got the better of her and she edged out the door. Lana rose to intervene in case Tammy intended to hurt Grizzly, but Grizzly's quiet woofle went on, and soon Lana heard Tammy's voice soften as she whispered to Grizzly: "I'm scared. I'm lonely. Nobody wants me. Nobody likes me."

For two years Lana and Grizzly visited the troubled girl every other week. When Tammy was rough, Grizzly moved away with quiet dignity. When she was sad, he lay beside her and woofed with understanding. Tammy would not or could not tell her therapist what was troubling her, but she confided in Grizzly in such a way that the therapist overheard her and thus was able to help her.

Tammy still threw tantrums, but never around Grizzly. "His love seems to calm her," her therapist told Lana. "For the first time she's found a creature she can trust, and her behavior in general is beginning to improve."

Someone at the center happened to remark that Grizzly's eyes did not look quite right, which led Lana to take him to a veterinarian to be examined. It was thus she learned Grizzly had long been blind, probably, the doctor said, as a result of a blow to the head. Lana's thoughts leaped back to the night Jeremy died and Grizzly ran out of the house directly into the side of a passing car. Ever since then, she realized, Grizzly must have been seeing with his heart, not his eyes.

Recently Lana and Grizzly were honored guests at a dinner honoring volunteers at the children's center. After a program of songs by the children's chorus, Tammy stepped forward. Once slovenly, with unwashed hair and broken fingernails, she was now well groomed and no longer slouched but stood proudly as she thanked Lana and Grizzly for all they had done for her and the others, the difference the two of them together had made in the children's lives.

When it was Lana's turn to speak, she said: "Once there was a special boy named Jeremy and he had a special dog named Grizzly. Jeremy had to leave us, but before he did, he asked Grizzly and me to try to find a way to help other children. Jeremy would be so pleased tonight to know we've succeeded and that his good shepherd has been your good shepherd, too."

Saving Trouper

The baby raccoon, no bigger than a drowned kitten, was sprawled facedown in a puddle in the road. Pat Kelso-Condos, an animal control officer in West Orange, New Jersey, stopped her van to collect the body. She could guess what must have happened: recent heavy rains had caused flash flooding in the area and a mother raccoon decided to move her litter to a safer place; this little one fell behind and the mother abandoned him to save the others.

"Poor thing," Pat murmured as she bent to pick him up. She had a soft spot in her heart for raccoons. Because rabies was present in the area, local residents killed every one they saw, and Pat, understanding the slaughter but knowing much of it was needless, felt protective toward them.

With a towel covering her hand she grasped the tiny creature. A shudder ran through his body. "Hey, you're still alive," she said, marveling as water streamed from his fur and he drew a rasping breath. She rubbed him with the towel and gently wiped away the mucus welling from his eyes and nose. A rumbling sound started in the baby's throat. Raccoons can purr like a cat, and Pat realized that was what this small creature was trying to do. He opened his eyes and looked up at her. If he'd spoken aloud, his plea couldn't have been clearer: *Please help me.*

Pat, a former veterinary technician, made an educated guess about the baby's condition—not rabies but probably distemper and certainly pneumonia. The breath gurgling through the fluid in his lungs sounded like a child blowing bubbles in a glass of milk. Pat guessed he might live minutes, a few hours at most.

The town had no facility for boarding wild animals. Pat's orders were to trap and release the healthy ones in a suitable area and destroy the ill and badly injured. But the appeal in this little one's eyes made her hesitate. She decided to take him home with her. There she dried him with a hair dryer, force-fed him a tiny bit of formula and laid him in a nest of towels under a heat lamp. At midnight she succeeded in getting a few more drops of formula into him. In the morning he was still alive.

"You're a trouper," she told him, impressed that as small and ill as he was, the baby was keeping up the battle to breathe. "If you're going to fight so hard to live, I've got to try to get you some help."

Many veterinarians are averse to treating wild animals, but Dr. Sharri Hill of the Animal Emergency Group in West Caldwell, New Jersey, was as touched by the little creature as Pat had been. She administered antibiotics and subcutaneous fluid and gave Pat a supply of both so she could continue to doctor the infant on her own. With her pen poised to fill out a chart, Dr. Hill paused at the first line. "What'll I put down for a name?"

"Trouper," said Pat, "because he's such a gutsy little fellow."

"Gutsy or not, I'm afraid his chances of making it are zero to none," the vet warned. "Raccoons very seldom survive distemper."

"Yes, I know," Pat said. "But I don't want to give up until he does."

Pat decided to ask her friends at the Wildlife Way Station in a nearby town if they would take him, because it was likely they would be able to do more for him than she could. She had to wait until evening to make the call because the two animal rehabilitators who had founded the facility worked at other jobs during the day, Andrea Abramson as director of the East Campus of Kean College, Freda Remmers as a teacher of communications at the college. When Pat reached Andrea, she described Trouper and his condition.

Andrea listened, then explained their situation. That day a possum hit by a car had been taken by the driver to the nearest vet. The vet had gotten hold of Freda, who stood by and pulled thirteen babies from the mother's pouch as the vet euthanized the severely injured mother. This meant that Andrea and Freda had thirteen infant possums who had to be bottle-fed every two hours. "Not only that," Andrea said, "but Boomer's back."

Pat remembered Boomer, who'd been everybody's favorite because even for a raccoon he was unusually smart. He'd learned to open a sliding glass door by watching Andrea and Freda do it, and he was great at tracking down treats hidden in their pockets. Months after he'd been released to the wild, he returned one brilliant moonlit night and his booming voice rang out. Freda and Andrea stepped outside, and there Boomer stood, a female raccoon beside him. "Look at that," Freda whispered. "He's brought his girl home to meet his mothers."

But this time he'd come back for help. He called to them, and when they went out, they saw that one of his front legs was bloody and mangled, the bone broken in several places. Raccoons can be vicious and Boomer was obviously in great pain, but they didn't need their thick leather gauntlets to pick him up because he remembered how they'd cared for him before and he trusted them utterly.

They took him to veterinarian Barry Orange, who opened the leg from paw to shoulder to piece the smashed bone back together, using wires and pins to hold it in place. So many stitches were needed to close the leg up again that Boomer looked like a sewing machine had run over him. The leg couldn't be put in a cast because Boomer, like any self-respecting raccoon, would have gone right to work to chew it off.

"So," Andrea finished her story, "Freda and I are taking turns sitting up with him during the night to distract him if he starts pulling at the stitches. Luckily, we can do that and feed the possum babies at the same time. But it doesn't sound like your little fellow is going to make it anyway, so if you could keep him, it would really be a help."

In the next days mucus continued to pour from Trouper's nose and eyes. Wheezing and rattling, he struggled to suck in air and grew ever thinner and more dehydrated. But still he clung to life. Pat put tiny dabs of Nutri-Cal on her finger and waited patiently until

Trouper could summon the strength to lick them off. She kept him wrapped in a blanket, and he told her by his efforts to purr that he liked her to hold him.

After four days, Pat picked up another raccoon, and her partner also brought one in. Since distemper is highly contagious and she had no facilities for isolating Trouper, she felt that now she had to take him to the Wildlife Way Station. With her husband driving and Pat keeping the tiny bundle warm inside her coat, they delivered Trouper to Andrea and Freda.

"I've seen dish mops with more life in them," Andrea commented when they handed him over. "You do know his chances are about one percent?"

"That's better than zero, which is what they were the last time I asked."

Andrea and Freda put Trouper in a cat carrier that was half on, half off a heating pad so he could have warmth if he needed it or crawl to the other side if it grew too hot for him. They started him on antibiotic injections and every four hours filled a syringe with hydrating fluid and Esbilac, a puppy milk replacement, and dripped it, drop by painstaking drop, into his mouth.

Even two rooms away and with the doors closed, Trouper's labored breathing was audible. The vet prescribed a bronchodilator. They crushed the pill and put it in the Esbilac. Trouper refused to swallow. They put it in Nutri-Cal, which he liked, but he refused to lick that. The only way they could get the pill into him was to put it in a pill popper, shoot it into the back of his mouth and hold his jaws closed until the pill went down his throat.

Every two hours either Freda or Andrea held the little dab of fur by the hind legs, turned him upside down and thumped him on his back and chest. The mucus poured out. They wiped it away with tissues. Soon his nose was raw. They coated the tissues with aloe vera. After every thumping session, as weak as he was, Trouper opened his eyes to look for his treat of Nutri-Cal.

Every evening Pat called to ask how Trouper was. Every evening the answer was the same: "He's still alive. Just." But after three weeks Andrea thought she detected a slight improvement. She put a dab of Nutri-Cal in a dish and set the dish near Trouper. He lifted his head and sniffed. Wobbling from side to side, he inched his way out of the towel-lined bowl that was his nest and licked the dish clean. That night when Pat called, Andrea said, "I think maybe your baby is going to win his fight."

"I knew he was a trouper!" Pat cried.

Soon, whenever Freda or Andrea came into the room, Trouper tottered to the door of the carrier and waited expectantly to be picked up, thumped, held and fed. Ordinarily the rehabilitators took pains to keep the animals from bonding with them, but with Trouper needing so much attention, they had no choice but to handle him. And handling led to fondling since he obviously loved having his ears scratched and responded with loud purrs when they talked to him.

After six weeks of treatment Trouper's breathing became less labored and his fur began to develop a sheen. He was kept on antibiotics for two more weeks to make sure the pneumonia had truly cleared, but then the little raccoon developed asthma. Again the rehabilitators despaired of his life until they noticed that the attacks occurred mainly when Andrea entered the room. It had been Andrea who had provided most of the two months of almost hourly handling that Trouper required, which meant that, as far as Trouper was concerned, Andrea was his mother, and when he saw her, he became so excited that he wheezed and choked.

As wrenching as it was to give up handling and petting the affectionate creature, it was clearly time to begin weaning him from human contact. They gave him a stuffed animal, which he took into his nest and slept with. As he became stronger, he began playing with it, challenging it to fight and giving it ferocious shakes. He was practicing the moves needed to survive in the wild, just as a baby raccoon would do with his littermates. When he wasn't pouncing on the plush toy, he talked to it, developing the vocalizations raccoons use to communicate with each other.

As it happened, another young raccoon also without a family arrived at the Wildlife Way Station about this time. Rocky had been an illegal family pet and needed to be trained for survival before he could be released; otherwise, it was likely that he would walk up to humans expecting to be petted and might instead be clubbed because people would assume he was attacking. After he had been quarantined sufficiently long for Andrea and Freda to be certain he was healthy, he and Trouper were moved together to an outdoor cage. The cage was as big as a walk-in closet and had wire mesh sides, a clip lock on the door because raccoons are clever enough to open any ordinary latch and a nesting box high up in a corner. Their first encounter was noisy as the two of them threatened each other with violence, but when their territorial disputes had been settled, they quickly became fast friends. Now each had a live partner to practice getting along with in the wild.

Because raccoons are nocturnal, Trouper and Rocky slept in their nesting box through the days. They roused enough to peek out when Freda stepped into the cage to clean it and bring them food, but then their bright, inquisitive faces vanished from the hole and they returned to their napping. When it was Andrea, however, Trouper swung out of the box onto a high shelf and walked along it until he was beside her and could lean forward to have his ears scratched.

But she never held him, fondled him or called him by name anymore. It tugged at her heart, but both she and Freda had worked hard to save his life, and she wanted Trouper to have every chance at surviving when he was released into the wild.

Is it worth going to the lengths they did just to save the life of an animal? Is it worth the considerable expense? Andrea and Freda support the Wildlife Way Station with their salaries from the college. It was their time and money that went into the training required to become licensed wildlife rehabilitators, their time and money that goes into saving the lives of some three hundred squirrels, rabbits, woodchucks, skunks and raccoons each year. Why do they do it?

They do it because they believe that all life on this planet is an interconnected web, and when they come upon a rent in that web, they want to do what they can to mend it. And they do it for the sake of a day like one the following spring when they took Trouper and Rocky some miles away to the property of friends where there were woods and fields and streams.

They set the animal carrier down at the edge of the woods, unbolted the door and crossed the field, back to where they'd left the car. Freda got in the driver's seat but Andrea continued to stand there, looking back at the carrier. After a while, Rocky nosed open the door, surveyed the field, tested to see if he really was free and made a dash for the woods. Trouper, half in, half out of the carrier, watched him go, then slowly turned this way and that, his eyes searching the field back and forth, back and forth. He took two steps out of the carrier, just enough to look over the top of it, and was looking there when Andrea, the width of the field away, brushed a gnat away. The movement caught Trouper's eye. He moved free of the carrier, sat up on his haunches and fixed his eyes on Andrea. Andrea ducked out of sight behind the car, and still he watched. Minute after minute went by.

"Get in the car," Freda told her. "Trouper's not going to move as long as you're here."

Reluctantly Andrea agreed. She moved back into view, stood for a moment, then waved goodbye.

They were told later by the friends whose property it was that twice Rocky reappeared and called to Trouper, but not until more than an hour had passed did Trouper turn and follow him into the woods.

The Pig Who Loved People

The phone rang at Bette and Don Atty's house in Johnstown, New York. A friend was calling to ask if they'd like to have a miniature pig.

"His name is Lord Bacon. He's four months old, and he's smarter than any dog," the friend told Don. "He loves people, and with Bette at home all the time I thought she might like company."

For a year Don had stood by helplessly as his wife struggled with agoraphobia, a fear of open spaces and crowds, apparently triggered by stress at work. Even after Bette had quit her job and was working at home as a freelance accountant, she suffered an incapacitating attack of anxiety just from going to the local mall. She never left the house now unless Don was with her.

Bette, when Don relayed the friend's offer to give them the pig, shook her head. "Think about it a minute," Don urged. "It might be good for you to have a pet."

Bette recalled reading in one of the many psychology books she had consulted about her condition that caring for another creature strengthens a person's inner being. But could a pig help her nerves?

"All right," she said reluctantly. "I guess a farmer will take him if we have to get rid of him."

Lord Bacon was fourteen inches high and twenty-four inches long, weighed forty-five pounds and was shaped like a root beer keg on stilts, they discovered when he arrived. Don laughed when he saw him: "That snout looks like he ran into a wall doing ninety!" Bette remarked, "I've got an old hairbrush with better-looking bristles than his."

The cage was opened and Lord Bacon trotted out wagging his tail. He looked around and headed for Bette. She knelt to greet him. He heaved himself up on his hind legs, laid his head on her shoulder and kissed her on the cheek with his leathery snout. For the first time in a long time Bette smiled.

The pig bustled about, exploring the house. He sat up on his broad bottom and begged for a treat. He gently chewed on Don's beard when Don put him on his lap. When Don or Bette whistled, the pig came to them, and when it was bedtime, he tried to follow them upstairs. With his potbelly he couldn't negotiate the steps, and Bette made up a bed for him in the kitchen, then sat on the floor and stroked him. "It's all right, Lord Bacon. We'll be here in the morning," she promised.

The next morning, instead of dreading having to face another day, Bette was eager to see her new pet. Lord Bacon scrambled to greet her and rubbed against her leg, which was like being massaged with a scouring pad. From then on, Bette was destined always to have a red rash of affection on her leg.

After breakfast the pig followed Bette into the home office, where she prepared tax returns, and settled down beside her desk. Bette found that when she grew edgy, if she reached down and petted Lord Bacon and said a few words, it made her feel calmer. When it was clear that the office was where the pig would be spending his days, Don brought home a doggie bed to put next to Bette's desk. Lord Bacon looked it over and decided that, with some alteration, it would do nicely. He planted his hoofs, ripped open the tartan pillow, pulled out the stuffing and then crawled inside the cover, content.

In the evenings, when Bette and Don drew up their armchairs to watch television, the pig pushed a chair over with his snout, sat on the floor in front of it and watched the figures on the screen, his head bobbing from side to side. Because they soon discovered he disliked loud noises, they kept the sound turned low. In her office Bette's phone hung on a post beside the desk, and Lord Bacon figured out that it stopped ringing when Bette picked it up. If Bette wasn't there to answer it immediately, he yanked the receiver off the hook, stood over it and grunted into the mouthpiece.

I wonder what my clients must think, Bette thought, half amused but a little embarrassed by the possibility that her clients assumed it was she doing the grunting.

A client came to see her about his tax return and was so charmed by her pet that he asked to bring his children to meet him. Soon other children were stopping by to see Lord Bacon. Finding this to be too serious a name for such a friendly pig, the kids took to calling him Pigger. The name stuck, and Pigger he was from then on.

The first time several people crowded into her office, Bette felt herself growing tense. Soon realizing, however, that they were too fascinated by the pig to pay any attention to her, she relaxed and enjoyed the company.

"It's fun coming home from work now," Don told Bette. "The first thing you say is, 'Guess what Pigger did today. He pulled the blankets off the bed,' or whatever, and we get to laughing and it feels like when we were first married."

"It wasn't so funny this morning when he locked me out of the house," Bette grumbled, but not very seriously. Pigger, following Bette in and out of the house, had watched her close the door behind her, and the next time he went in he did the same. The only problem was, the door was on the latch and Bette was still outside. Luckily, a spare key was hidden in the backyard.

Pigger was a superb mimic, and Bette found he would imitate whatever she did. If she shook her head, Pigger would shake his. If she twirled, Pigger would twirl. Soon Bette was teaching tricks to her pig that few dogs are smart enough to learn. Her father tried to persuade her to bring Pigger to a senior citizens' gathering to entertain them. Bette demurred. "Pigger can run like the wind and feint like a soccer player," she said. "If he gets away from me, I won't be able to catch him, and I can't put him on a leash because he plants his feet and refuses to walk. I'd look pretty silly, wouldn't I, a grown lady dragging a pig?"

The next evening Don came home with a baby stroller. "What's that for?" Bette demanded.

"It's a pigmobile, so you can take Pigger to the seniors' meeting." He lifted Pigger into the stroller, and Pigger sat up in it, a blanket around his shoulders, a green visor on his head. As Don pushed him about, it was clear that Pigger loved it, so Bette agreed to take him to meet the seniors.

Her nerves tightened as she drove up to the building. She turned off the motor and sat in the car trembling. She stroked Pigger, seat-belted beside her, and felt calmer. *I've got to conquer my fears,* she told herself. *I can't spend the rest of my life being afraid.* She struggled out, settled Pigger in the pigmobile and wheeled him into the building.

The seniors were intrigued. "What is *that?*" they asked. Bette lifted Pigger to the floor. He immediately singled out the oldest woman in the place and trotted over to nuzzle her cheek. The seniors broke into laughter and crowded around to pet him. Bette answered their questions, at first haltingly, then with enthusiasm. She told the seniors that pigs are smarter than dogs and twice as clean: "Pigger loves it when I put him in the bathtub for a good scrub." To show off how smart he was, she called to Pigger and told him he was a handsome hog. Pigger strutted about proudly. Then she scolded him for being piggy. Pigger lowered his head in shame and, for good measure, let his tongue hang out. His audience laughed and cheered.

Word got around about the clever pig, and soon Bette and Pigger were going on what Don called their "pig gigs." At a nursing home, Bette wheeled Pigger from room to room to visit with the patients. In one room, an old woman was sitting staring at her hands clenched in her lap. Suddenly her head came up and her face cracked in the beginnings of a smile. She held out her hands, then wrapped her arms around herself. An aide whispered to Bette that the woman had not smiled, spoken or taken an interest in anything since her husband's death some months before. "What is it?" Bette asked. "Do you want to hug him?" As Bette picked up Pigger and held him so the old woman could pet him, Pigger stayed perfectly still, his ears cocked and his mouth drawn up in a grin.

On later visits, when Pigger came through the front door in his pigmobile, the call would go out: "Pigger's here!" A commotion would start in the halls—the squeak of wheelchairs, the *tap-tap* of walkers, the shuffle of slippered feet—as the residents hurried to talk to him and pet him. The more Bette saw of sick and helpless people, the more thoughts of her own illness faded away. "I used to hate myself," she told Don, "but now I'm beginning to thank God every day for being me. Pigger is making me well."

It occurred to Bette that Pigger could carry a message to school-children, and she began to take him into classrooms. She invited the children to ask Pigger if he would ever take drugs. Pigger shook his head emphatically while grunting and snorting with disgust at the idea. Asked if he'd stay in school and study hard, Pigger bowed low and nodded solemnly. The kids wanted to know what Pigger liked to eat. "Dog biscuits, of course," Bette told them. "Also beans, corn, carrots, apples and Cheerios. But the two things Pigger loves best are popcorn and ice cream. At the Dairy Queen he gets his own dish of ice cream and eats it neatly from a spoon."

The kids' comments about Pigger ranged from "He feels like a pot scrubber" to "He has cute ears" to "He looks like my uncle." One little boy, hugging Pigger, said wistfully, "I wish you could come home with me. I know you'd love me." Bette had to grip Pigger's collar tightly to keep him from following the boy.

Sometimes Bette and Don would be shopping in the supermarket and from the next aisle a child's voice would ring out: "There's the pig's mother and father!" An embarrassed parent would be dragged over to be introduced to "the pig's family."

When strangers stopped, stared and inquired what Pigger was, Don answered, "To us, he's a pig, but to him, he's people." Occasionally he quoted Winston Churchill: "Dogs look up to us. Cats look down on us. Pigs treat us as equals." And Pigger would confirm this by grunting.

By the end of a year, Pigger and Bette had made ninety-five public appearances, and Bette was handling the occasions with poise and flair. In July, Pigger was invited to attend the annual Fulton County senior citizens' picnic. The day before was hot, and Bette opened the back door. "Why don't you go out and cool off in your pool, Pigger?" she suggested.

Pigger trotted into the yard and Bette went back to work. Something prompted her to check on him half an hour later. He was lying in his favorite napping spot in the shade of a barberry bush, but Bette thought he seemed unnaturally still. She went to him. He wasn't breathing.

Panic engulfed Bette and she began to wail. *No, I mustn't carry on. Pigger doesn't like loud noises.* She went in the house and called a friend to come be with her until Don got home. Then she knew she was going to make it.

Pigger had succumbed to a pulmonary aneurysm, but Bette has her own explanation of why he died. "Pigger had a heart so big, it burst with all the love in it." She goes on to say, "He not only helped me become my old self, he brightened so many other lives, too. He was a wonderful friend. There will never be another Pigger."

Afterword:
The Year of Pure Love

Why do people become devoted to an animal, sometimes with an intensity that is startling? The recent loss of a cat I held dear has made me ponder the reasons. Why did I love Bitty so much? Why do I mourn him so fiercely?

It was a year ago that I found him. A friend and I had gone for a walk on the mountain road, with my dog, Freebie, in the lead. Suddenly, with loud, glad cries, a kitten rushed from a roadside thicket and ran straight to Freebie. The dog was too surprised to bark or back off as the kitten reared up on his hind legs and butted Freebie's chin while uttering delighted sounds at having found company. Well nourished and neat, the kitten had obviously not been out in the winter cold long, which suggested he'd dashed, unnoticed, out a briefly opened door of one of the houses within walking distance. We picked him up and set about returning him to his owner.

"No," we were told at one house after another. "No, it's not our kitten. Thanks anyway."

When we'd run out of houses and with the twilight smelling of snow soon to fall, there was nothing to do but tuck the kitten into my down jacket and carry him home—not to keep, because I already had two cats, but to shelter until he could be taken to the Humane Society the next day. We were amused as we traveled down the mountain that the kitten, his head resting on the jacket's zipper, never stopped talking. His animated cries were not miaows and there was no note of distress in them. Indeed, they sounded like a joyous "wow," sometimes pronounced exuberantly, sometimes interrogatively, sometimes, as though he were a rock singer, broken into two or three syllables. He uttered these "wows" as he looked at whoever was speaking, quite as though he intended them as his contribution to the conversation.

At the house he kept up a running commentary as he met the resident cats, had some cold chicken for supper and explored the house. Even after I'd settled him in the kitchen in a towel-lined wicker basket on top of a chest, his head popped up whenever the volume of the conversation changed, and he added his cheerful opinion.

So endearing was his insistence on communicating that by morning the projected trip to the Humane Society had somehow become an excursion to the vet instead to check the kitten's health and sex preparatory to keeping him. Despite appearances and the kitten's young age, I had begun to believe that he was a female and in heat, else why was he so vocal? But the vet scotched this theory, pronouncing him male, about nine weeks old and in perfect condition, without a mite in his ear or a flea in his coat.

"So," I said as the kitten rode home beside me on the front seat, his paws neatly tucked under, "you're just a very talkative little bit of a cat."

"Wow-ow," he agreed cheerily.

After that, his name was Little Bit for a while; then it became Bitty.

I, who had always been partial to longhairs with plumed tails and pantalooned rumps, thought Bitty not ugly—it's a rare cat who is really ugly—but uninteresting-looking. He was a tabby, a domestic shorthair—a generic cat, as a friend described him—with stripes of darkness in his brindle coat, white paws and a rather too pointed face. In his favor was that he was spotless and his eyes were vigilant with love and interest in the world. He was not so much curious as participatory, eager to assist at all openings of doors, boxes, letters and grocery bags, and choosing always to sleep, if he had a choice, in arms or a lap, under bedcovers against a back or, in the absence of a human body, between Freebie's front paws.

He was never demanding, always equable, never frightened, always cheerful. Even when lugged around throughout an entire day by a visiting seven-year-old nephew, he did not complain. He played a number of invented games with Freebie, who adored him. He did not sharpen his claws on the furniture and sat on the velvet chairs only when I wasn't home. Whenever I walked into a room where he was asleep, he immediately roused himself to say hello, and no matter how tired he was from roaming in the fields, he welcomed being picked up and hugged. Affectionate, responsive, loving and communicative, he was the perfect cat.

At least I thought so, and when he disappeared, I was heartbroken. I had had guests for dinner one Saturday night, and he nipped through the door when they departed. It was the kind of night irresistible to a cat. A huge moon bathed the meadow across the way in white light and black shadows, so it was fruitless to try to call him back, and anyway, he often enough spent a night in the fields and in the morning was waiting on the front porch to be let in for breakfast.

But on Sunday morning he wasn't on the porch. I began calling and soon went looking for him. I searched up and down the road, in the first field across the road, in the second field, in the copse that separates them, along the broad path that once was a single-line railroad. I asked at the barn where thoroughbred trotters are stabled and at the houses within any conceivable distance. I searched and called and listened for his answering "wow-ow," growing more and more alarmed until my fear was like a great gray sack of feathers weighing down my back.

Chester, a cat I'd had before Bitty, had been savaged by a raccoon. Had Bitty met a similar fate? I hunted for him frantically. If only I could come upon him still alive, I would somehow manage to save him, I was sure. But after four days, when I gave up hope because the nights had turned bitter and he wouldn't have been able to survive in such cold, I longed to come across any clue to his fate. I dreaded finding a scrap of fur, a gnawed leg bone, a mangled body, but I could scarcely bear not knowing what had happened to him.

I didn't find a clue. It has been months now and still I grieve, still I cannot look out the front door without the foolish hope that a generic-looking cat will be sitting on the porch with his paws tucked under and that I will hear that inimitable voice say, "Wow?"

The depth of my pain has made me think about my year with Bitty. We never quarreled, never disagreed, never got on each other's nerves as people sometimes do. We had nothing to hold against each other, no residue of bitterness, no unhealed wounds. I had never scolded; he had never let me down. I had never been impatient; he had never pushed me away. It had been a year of pure love.

As I thought about this year of pure love, I wondered if it wasn't at least part of the reason an animal can become so important in one's life. Pure love is rare among humans. I have loved and been loved in my life, sometimes deeply, but never without reserve; there were always strings, caveats. I see now that that is almost inevitable in human love, and not only inevitable but desirable. A constant problem for every human being is to feel close enough to another to stave off fear of aloneness and distant enough from that same other to maintain the boundaries of the self. One must not engulf and must equally avoid being swallowed up.

But that's not a problem with an animal. It doesn't feel the least bit threatening to be boundlessly loved by a dog or cat, and the dog or cat is more than content to be boundlessly loved in return. It doesn't interfere with his individuality or autonomy. He'll go right on being an animal, his own animal, no matter how much affection is lavished on him. Thus, a human has carte blanche to love a pet at the top of his bent, just as fully, generously, wholeheartedly as he is capable of, and that is a superbly satisfying thing—to live out one's feelings without reserve.

Human love is, in Donald Barthelme's description, both "grisly and golden." How relaxing it is, then, to experience the simplicity of loving an animal. You don't have to worry that the love might not be returned fully enough or that it might be returned too fully. You can love a pet without worries about the quality of the love, without judgments, without agendas. It is, as it was with Bitty, pure love, a confirmation of one's capacity to love and a relief from the complications of human love.

Those complications—and so much else—one is always trying to put into words. Bitty had only his one word, "wow," the volume and resonance of which he varied to suit the situation, his need of the moment, and the feeling he wished to express. And again that very simplicity was relaxing. How good it is not to have to hunt for the right words, to communicate without the barrier of words. An aunt of mine had a passion for tiny babies, and I understand it now—the holding in your arms of a small, warm body, the conveying of love and reassurance by comforting, wordless sounds, the absolute being there for another living being.

There is, as well, the tactile pleasure of closeness. With Bitty sleeping in my lap while I read or watched television, I let my fingers wander in his fur and enjoyed the velvety feel. He would grow heavier and heavier as he sank into deep sleep, and that, too, would enlist my heart, for it spoke of profound trust. Bitty trusted as I don't suppose any person ever has or ever could. It didn't occur to him that I might hurt, frighten or reject him. He utterly assumed that I always wanted him in my lap, which I sometimes didn't, although I never let him know it, because I never wanted him to feel that his companionship, so freely offered, was not as freely welcomed.

Companionship—that is, I suppose, the single word most often used when people try to explain their attachment to a pet. The companionship has the inestimable value of being able to be bought and, although purchased, willingly given. Unless an animal is badly mistreated—and sometimes even then—its devotion can be counted on. A young man who walks with his dog on the road past my house often stops to chat if I am working in the garden, and while we talk, Lucy, his mongrel dog, never takes her eyes off his face. She listens so attentively to his tone of voice that she moves to his side when he starts to say goodbye. I don't know this man's story except that he lives alone in a house in the woods, and while I might wish for him some human companionship, I know he is safe in the world and connected because he has Lucy.

The acceptance of a person by an animal is unconditional. I have a ninety-year-old friend who recently had to have her ancient dog put down. Over her protests that she was a lifelong dog person, I took her to the Humane Society to adopt a kitten. She picked out a friendly, orange-colored cat who immediately set about becoming as attached to a ninety-year-old as he would have to a nine-year-old. Animals have no preconceived notion of what an owner should look like or be like; they have no age or sex preferences. Whatever your looks, gifts or assets, or lack of them, "they ask no questions," as George Eliot noted, "they pass no criticisms." They accept the owner they get and, if treated kindly, are deliciously satisfied.

Incidentally, this erstwhile dog person claims the kitten has changed her life. When I telephone, she doesn't wait to hear what I've called about but starts right in: "I'm absolutely dotty about that kitten! He's wonderful! He follows me everywhere. He talks to me." Her enthusiasm for life, which had dimmed, is once again bright, not just because of the kitten's companionship but because once more she has something that needs her. Erik Erikson described the mature stage of life as characterized by "generativity," the drive to nurture, protect and enable the small and the dependent. It is the need to be needed. We all experience it, and animals allow us to express it long after children are grown and gone.

The animal who is looked after returns the favor, not in kind, but by reminding us of some important truisms about life. One is to live in the present moment. We muse about yesterday—what was said or done or left undone—or the far yesterdays of roads taken or not taken, chances missed, loves lost. We think about tomorrow—plans, dates, hopes, worries. What we don't exist in, at least not nearly often enough, is *now*. We are always looking backward or forward, forgetting to notice this moment, this time, forgetting to enjoy *now*.

Bitty made me conscious of this. He would seek out and luxuriate in the one patch of sunlight on the kitchen floor, enjoying what the present had to offer to its fullest. Seeing him made me remind myself to "be here now"—feel the sun, taste the food, listen to the music, hear the words.

Animals put us in touch with the basics, with the natural world, which has little to do with get, spend, consume, throw away. They are a bridge to the natural world. Searching for Bitty in the field, I moved from the periphery, where I ordinarily walked, into the center. There I discovered in the stiff winter weeds an area laced with byways; some of the paths, as crooked as capillaries, ended in cul-de-sacs, some in piazzas of flattened grasses where deer bedded down, some in burrows from field mouse to woodchuck size. Was Bitty even now at the bottom of one of those burrows, dragged there by a creature bigger, stronger, more predatory than he?

Should I, foreseeing this might happen, have prevented Bitty from commuting between the human and animal worlds? I think not. As there is a dark side to nature, there is a dark side to human nature, a side that likes to control, dominate, lord it over the animals. They are in our power, and it is always tempting to exercise power when we have it. It is a temptation to be resisted. Just as much as is consonant with reasonable safety, I think an animal should be free to run, climb, stalk, bask, dig, wander—not if he lives in the city, obviously, but if his home is in a place where this is feasible. It is perfectly possible that I am wrong about this— many people would say so—but I have always felt that it is more to the point to be happy than to be safe. Life is risky, and you are most alive when you have the most at risk. People put themselves in jeopardy mountain climbing, speed racing or deep-sea diving for the extreme joy of surviving the dangers. Why shouldn't an animal have the same thrill?

I could not deny it to Bitty, who loved the wild. If I had it to do over again, would I still have the courage to let him roam free? Perhaps if I knew I was going to lose him after only a year, no. But there will be another kitten one day, and when he is old enough, I'll let him wander the fields if that is his pleasure because animals, like humans, need to follow their bliss if they are to get the deepest enjoyment from life and find the deepest meaning in it.

Friends knowing my grief over the loss of Bitty say, "That's why I don't have a pet anymore. It hurts too much when you lose it." It does hurt. But which is worse: the tragedy of a loss or the emptiness of having all that love inside you and nothing to give it to?

Having is best. Having had is second best. Never having had at all is less than a distant third; it doesn't place at all. If I had said "I cannot go through this hurt again" when Katie died or Chester was killed by the raccoon or Freebie had the stroke, I would have missed this year of pure love with Bitty.

"Tenderness and absolute trust and communication and truth: these things matter more and more as one grows older," writes a character in Iris Murdoch's novel *The Sea, the Sea.* I believe it to be so. I also believe these things are hard to find, except partially, in other people—and hard to bestow on other people, at least in the full, easy measure implied. As our bodies collect debits as we grow older, so do we collect psychological scar tissue, which gets in the way of tenderness and trust and communication and truth. But not in relation to an animal. I never said a cross word to Bitty, never ignored or made fun of him, never did not respond, never failed to be loving. Although only a cat, Bitty let me be the person I could have been unfailingly if life experience hadn't gotten in the way.

Am I exaggerating? Yes, a little. Perhaps a lot. Pets do not provide a full life, only make life fuller. However grisly relationships with other people may be, they are still golden and immensely necessary. An animal does not substitute for them, and I have not meant to imply that they do. I have only tried to explore why I and the people in the accounts in this book became so involved with an animal, went so far out of our way, cared so much.

We may belong to what has occasionally and derogatively been called "the mafia of animal lovers," but we have our reasons.